Revised Edition

Acting for Animators

A Complete Guide to Performance Animation

D1308851

Ed Hooks

Foreword by Brad Bird

Illustrations by Paul Naas

HEINEMANN
Portsmouth, NH

Heinemann
A division of Reed Elsevier Inc.
361 Hanover Street
Portsmouth, NH 03801–3912
www.heinemanndrama.com

Offices and agents throughout the world

© 2003, 2000 by Ed Hooks

Library of Congress Cataloging-in-Publication Data
Hooks, Ed.
  Acting for animators : a complete guide to performance animation / Ed Hooks ;
  foreword by Brad Bird ; illustrations by Paul Naas. — Rev. ed.
      p. cm.
  ISBN 0-325-00580-X (alk. paper)
  1. Animation (Cinematography). 2. Motion picture acting.   I. Title.
TR897.5.H66 2003
791.43'7—dc21   2003007225

Editor: Lisa A. Barnett
Production editor: Sonja S. Chapman
Electronic product developers: Dan Breslin and Eyeon Interactive
Cover and text illustrations: Paul Naas
Cover design: Catherine Hawkes, Cat & Mouse
Compositor: Reuben Kantor, QEP Design
Manufacturing: Steve Bernier

Printed in the United States of America on acid-free paper
07   06   05   VP   3   4   5

For Ken Bielenberg, who first asked me,
"Would you be willing to teach acting
on-site? I work for an animation company."

Indeed, the more the arts develop the more they depend on each other for definition.

—E. M. Forster, *Aspects of the Novel*

Contents

Foreword

One never hears about how many tubes of paint Picasso used to create *Guernica*, the exact number of notes contained in Gershwin's "Rhapsody in Blue," or how many facial expressions Brando deployed in *On the Waterfront*.

Yet when the art of character animation is discussed at all, it is usually in mind-numbingly numeric terms, with statements along the lines of "more than 23 skadrillion drawings were used in the production of *Rumpelstiltskin*. If each drawing were laid end to end, they would reach to Jupiter and back 6.7 times."

When an art form is so consistently described in such a dreary way it's easy to see why animation is often thought to be more technique than art, and its practitioners little more than technicians with pencils (or clay or pixels or puppets) in the eyes of the public.

When an animated character breaks through and becomes part of the cultural landscape, the voice actor—not the animator—is credited, because people understand what a voice actor does.

A friend of mine supervised the animation of a lead character in a major animated feature. In many interviews the well-known actress who voiced the character immodestly claimed that the animators had simply, in effect, copied her mannerisms and performance. In reality the animators had found her acting style generic and boring, and had turned elsewhere for inspiration: to people they had known in their own lives, friends and members of their families, even to studying Julia Louis Dreyfuss in episodes of *Seinfeld*.

What is typically lost in discussions about animation is the fact that when you watch an animated film, the performance you're seeing is the one *the animator* is giving to you. If an animated character makes you laugh or cry, feel fear, anger, empathy, or a million other emotions, it is largely due to the work of these often unsung artists, who invest a lot of themselves in the creation of these indelible moments.

If the public could watch the faces of the best animators when caught up in the act of drawing an emotional scene, they would see artists as fully invested in *the moment* as the best live actors. The difference is that an animator *stays* in that moment, often working for weeks to express an emotion his or her character takes only seconds to convey onscreen. The art of character animation, then, is to try to catch lightning in a bottle one volt at a time.

Countless books have been dedicated to the graphics, the look, the techniques, the *process* of character animation, but precious little has been written about performance, which is nothing less than the heart of the matter. As with any art, the vast majority of animation is garbage. It overflows with "characters"—human and not, male, female, fat, thin, tall, short, young, old, and in-between; characters who possess different voices, different clothes, head shapes, skin color, hair color, characters that have in fact only one thing in common—they all move exactly alike.

Ed Hooks knows that in the very best animated films, movement defines character: Lady moves differently than Tramp, Woody moves differently than Buzz, and Wallace moves nothing like Gromit. By looking outside the medium itself, and by intelligently and thoughtfully examining character animation from an actor's perspective, Mr. Hooks has made a valuable contribution toward deepening our understanding of it.

I have no idea how many hours it took Mr. Hooks to write this book, how many gallons of ink was used in its printing, or how far it would stretch if you laid each copy of this edition end to end.

And I hope to God it never comes up.

Brad Bird

Acknowledgments

Though writing a book may be a singular activity, it is not something one does alone. Many talented and generous people in the world of animation have influenced me since I wrote the first edition of *Acting for Animators*. Their input has been occasionally extensive and intense and sometimes amounted to little more than a casual exchange of emails or maybe a passing comment in party conversation. Many have taken the time to dialogue with me in Internet news groups. Each person has been important and influential. I am not myself an animator and am therefore dependent on the goodwill, wisdom, and advice of professional animators. The more I understand about the magic that is done with animation, the better able I am to bring to bear what I understand about formal acting theory.

The list, though woefully incomplete, includes:

> Doug Aberle, Brad Bird, Marc Vulcano, Michael Barrier, Paul Naas, Sven Pannicke, Brad Blackbourn, John Canemaker, Tien Yang, Jeff Cooperman, Keith Lango, Phil Tippett, Rex Grignon, Angie Jones, Mike Caputo, Alberto Menache, Larry Bafia, Jean Newlove, Leslie Bishko, Matt Brunner, Rachelle Lewis, Peter Plantec, and Siobhan Fenton.

On the editorial side, I would be remiss if I didn't acknowledge the invaluable contributions of Lisa Barnett, senior editor at Heinemann. Many publishers turned down *Acting for Animators* before it reached Heinemann. The typical rejection response was, "If there was a need for animators to have a book about acting, there would already be one." The publishers simply didn't believe me. Then, in a leap of calculated faith, Lisa gave this book the green light. Without her endorsement and the financial commitment of Heinemann, it is likely you would not be reading these words right now. I am proud and honored to be working with this fine company that has since published another of my books, *Acting Strategies for the Cyber Age*.

And finally, thanks to my wife, Cally, and our daughter, Dagny. They are now and forever the twin animated beacons in my life. I am continually inspired and oriented by their light.

Introduction

My first class with animators took place one sunny afternoon in April 1996, at Pacific Data Images, Palo Alto, California. I had at that point been a professional actor and acting teacher for twenty years, but I knew nothing about animation. When I introduced myself to the assembled PDI animators that day, I had not yet drawn a distinction between the way that animators perceive and apply acting theory and the way that stage actors perceive and apply it. I erroneously believed that there was only one way to learn acting, and that was to get up on your feet and act. That first day I brought with me a box of scripts from Neil Simon stage comedies. I handed out scripts, assigned scenes, and instructed the animators on how to rehearse together outside of class.

When we gathered for class for week number two, I discovered that hardly anybody had rehearsed their scenes. If this had happened in one of my stage-acting classes, I would have hit the roof and lectured everybody about professionalism. At PDI, however, I realized right away that I was the one out of step, not the students. I was on their turf, and this was my first reality check. I took a deep breath and started trying to figure a way of teaching acting theory to people who did not themselves want to get up and act. Looking back on those early classes from my current perspective, I am astonished that the Human Resources people at PDI didn't send me packing. They didn't, thanks in large part to the endorsement of their visual effects genius Ken Beilenberg (Shrek and Shrek II), who had been a student in my regular stage-acting class and who first brought me to the company. "Ken says you're a good acting teacher, so if you're willing to try, then so are we," they told me at lunch. I will never be able to properly express my gratitude to them or to Ken for the opportunity.

I worked with the animators at PDI for some long weeks. We quit trying to do scene work right away, and I began lecturing on acting theory. I started considering more closely the connections between thinking, emotion, and physical action. I brought in clips from Charlie Chaplin movies and deconstructed them to display acting principles. I read The Illusion of Life (Thomas and Johnston 1981), and I convinced some of the animators to sit down with me to show me what they were doing. I designed some simple and fun improvisations to underline particular acting principles. I probably learned more than the animators did in this process and, once they went into production for their movie, *Antz*, the classes ended. I didn't work on the movie itself but, by then, my education about the animation process was underway and I was loving it. Because I had the good fortune of working with top-rung artists right out of the chute, other companies began calling me for acting classes. One workshop led to another and I continued to learn and tweak the content. With each class, I tried something new. That process has continued up to the present day. I'm still massaging the content, but now I have a firm grasp on the differences between the way that animators perceive and apply acting theory versus the way that stage actors perceive and apply it.

Viva la Difference!

A stage actor performs in the present moment, utilizing a process of rehearsed repetition. He learns the lines, plays actions, and tries not to anticipate what the upcoming moment holds. A stage actor is taught that indication (showing an audience how you feel) is an acting error. He learns to stay in the moment, playing off the reality of whatever his scene partners are doing. A stage actor's art requires that he be psychologically visible on stage. This is why acting classes for stage actors spend so much time on the challenge of removing emotional blocks.

An animator, by contrast, is taught to be an *expert* at indication. An animator's task is to specifically show an audience how the animated character feels. There is no way an animated character can play off the reality of his scene partner in the present moment because there is no present moment in animation. There is only an indication of a present moment (mocap and rotoscoping excluded). The very word *anticipation*, which is anathema to a stage actor, means something totally different and positive to the animator. For her, anticipation is a necessary part of her art. And, of course, an animator has no need to be psychologically visible, even though it may be a nice quality to have in life.

I have learned over time that acting training for animators needs to include zero exercises for releasing emotional blocks. An animator needs to know a lot about acting, but she doesn't need to know everything about it. She doesn't, for example, need to learn how to make herself cry on cue because, if she were to do that, she wouldn't be able to see to animate.

This revised second edition of *Acting for Animators* brings the reader up-to-date on my approach to acting as it is learned by animators. By the time you finish reading, you should have a working grasp of essential acting principles, some of which go back to Aristotle. This book will not teach you how to draw or manipulate pixels on a screen because I am not an animator. I cannot myself draw a credible image of a toaster! I'm presuming that my reader either already knows those skills or is currently being instructed by experienced animators. My goal is to interpret and filter the basic principles of acting so that you can apply them to animation. I have tried hard to make it brief and easy to digest. Acting is an art like music or ballet, but it ought to be fun.

A Brief History of Acting

The roots of acting are in shamanism. Seven thousand years ago there were nomadic tribes following the herds in Mesopotamia. A tribe would encounter a rough winter or a thinning herd and would call out its shaman who would paint himself blue, put on a mask, and chant to the animal or weather gods. The point of the exercise was to help the tribe get through another season and to survive.

By 50 B.C., when the Greek theatre arrived, the tribes still had shamans except that they were organized into choruses. There were regular Dionysus festivals in which the chorus chanted the Dithyramb. The enterprise was still shamanistic, but it had more structure than in ancient days. One day, a member of the chorus—Thespis—donned a mask, pretended to be a god, and spoke back to the chorus. Acting was born. Over the next couple of hundred years, the solo actor was joined by other actors (Aeschylus and Sophocles), and it evolved that the chorus was supporting the actors instead of the other way around. (The modern-day Broadway musical still fits this paradigm in fact.) Religious ceremonies morphed into drama as gods were replaced in the stories by demigods, human beings, and heroes. The stories shifted away from being about man's relationship with the gods and onto man's relationship with other men. Today, actors are still speaking to the tribe, still talking about how to get through a tough winter. When you or your character act, you are calling the tribe together. The tribe (audience) expects you to lead and to have something to say. That is the essence of the theatrical contract.

Animation Is Born

According to Donald Crafton in *Before Mickey—The Animated Film 1898–1929* (1982), Emile Cohl's 1908 "Fantasmagorie" was probably the very first animated cartoon. If true, then the animation industry today is less than one hundred years old. During this short time, we've gone through rubber hose animation, the birth of Mickey Mouse, *Three Little Pigs*, *Snow White*, the rise of CGI, *Toy Story*, and flirtation with photo-real. The technical standard in today's major studio releases is breathtaking. *Time* and *Newsweek* rapturously report on strides being made in the depiction of water, hair, fur, and skin.

Animation is poised on the brink of truly astounding advances. Computer graphics has largely overtaken hand-drawn animation in major feature films and on TV, bringing with it sky-high audience expectations. Seventy years ago, audiences would fill the seats just to watch animated characters like Gertie the Dinosaur who seemed to move across the screen. Today, audiences are not impressed that a character appears to have the illusion of life or that its gestures appear to be motivated. The standard that used to be almost magical is almost a yawn in the twenty-first century. Indeed, this is the great challenge and opportunity that is facing the industry.

Acting for Animators Versus Acting for Actors

Animators are oriented to what stage actors disparagingly call *results*. From a trained stage actor's perspective, the way animators come at the subject is upside down. An animator is concerned with whether a character's eyebrows should be raised to show curiosity, how many blinks occur in an excited moment, whether it is the head or the shoulders that first turns for a sideways glance, how to indicate emotion; actors, by contrast, think about such things rarely if ever because they are taught not to play results. Emotions and facial expressions are results of inner motivation. A stage actor strives to find intention and motivation, which manifest themselves in the actions, and he plays actions in pursuit of objectives. He is taught that whatever emotion and facial/body movement are appropriate to the moment will just naturally happen. If an actor in one of my stage-acting classes asked me if she should lift her eyebrows to suggest curiosity, I would be dumbfounded. Actors shouldn't be thinking about eyebrows! But animators ask these kinds of questions all the time, as well they should.

Professional acting training is a relatively recent development in history, dating back only to 1897, when Constantin Stanislavsky established his workshops at Russia's Moscow Art Theatre. It was he, under the influence of Freud and Pavlov, who fathered naturalistic, psychologically-based acting techniques. Remember Pavlov's famous experiment with the dog, the food, and the bell? Pavlov would ring a bell whenever he fed the dog so, after a while, the dog would salivate when he heard the bell, even if there was no food involved. Stanislavsky observed this behavior and asked himself why actors couldn't do that, too. Would it be possible to train actors to have an emotional reaction to something like a bell ringing? That was the basic idea behind Stanislavsky's work. Before his innovations, actors struck poses and "showed" the audience that they were experiencing emotion. The implied message to the audience was, "I'm not really feeling anything but, if I were, it would look like this." Stanislavsky said, "Let's really feel something instead of pretending to do so."

Prior to Stanislavsky, stage acting was learned mainly through a process of informal apprenticeship. An aspiring actor would present himself at the theatre door and ask for the opportunity to learn by doing. He would pull curtains, move props, carry spears in crowd scenes, paint flats, and generally sit at the master's knee, soaking up accumulated theatrical wisdom. When formal acting classes later took root in the United States and in England, the teachers were dependent on this same initiative on the part of the student actor. A student actor was one who wanted badly to be on the stage. In my stage-acting classes, I depend on the student to bring a certain initiative to the process. The students memorize scenes—mainly from stage plays—rehearse outside of class, and then present the scenes for critique, analysis, and re-work.

Since animators do not generally aspire to being on stage themselves, it is nonproductive for an acting teacher to expect them to rehearse and present scenes. Acting training for animators is training with a difference. It is more akin to acting training for writers or puppeteers. Animators need to have a seat-of-the-pants understanding of acting, but they learn it through observation, discussion, and example rather than workshop scene work and appearances in front of audiences.

Frankly, I think the acting that animators do is more difficult than what stage actors do. Stage actors work within the fleeting moment, moving from action to action, emotion to emotion, never looking back, never focusing on the emotion itself. A good animator must go through a similar process of motivating his characters on a moment-to-moment basis, but he then must keep re-creating that same moment over and over and over again, sometimes for weeks on end, while he captures it on the cell or computer screen. Actors learn that once a moment is gone, it's gone for good, but animators have to pitch camp at the intersection of movement and emotion. For the stage actor, it is an error to attempt re-creation of the performance he gave yesterday. For the animator, the ability to re-create—and describe—yesterday's performance is essential.

When a stage actor rehearses a show, he is not trying to get the performance to a point where it can be frozen and replayed on demand. He is connecting the emotional dots, finding through-lines in intention and objectives. The only thing that remains the same on a performance-to-performance basis is the blocking. This is why performances in the theatre are so unique. The audience and the actors get together in the same place at the same time and cocreate the performance. The play your friend saw last week will never be seen again. When you go see the same show on his recommendation, you'll see the same story and blocking, but a different performance. True, an actor's performance can be captured on film but even in that process, the acting happens in the present moment when it's being captured. If an actor does twenty "takes" on a given shot, they are going to be twenty different takes. On a moment-to-moment basis, nothing remains the same. The performance that was captured on film this morning is going to be different from the performance that is captured after lunch. Animators, comparatively speaking, operate in a much different kind of environment. This is why the "outtakes" that Pixar included at the conclusion of the *Toy Story* movies are so amusing. The entire idea of outtakes in animation is insane! That is a concept that only works with live action.

Seven Essential Acting Concepts
1

The late Shamus Culhane correctly pointed out in his wonderful book, *Animation from Script to Screen* (1990) that Disney-style realism is harder to accomplish than more restrictive, stylized cartoons. To adhere to realism is to abide by the laws of physics, weight, and volume. That's why, even if you do not aspire to realistic animation, it still is smart of you to learn what it's all about—and that is why, even though animation takes many different forms, I am mainly concerned with realism in this book. Picasso's earliest paintings were very realistic. Examine his *Nude Study of Jose Romain* (1895) and *Science and Charity* (1897), and you'll see realism worthy of Michelangelo. He could not have executed *Seated Old Man* (1970) or *Two Women of Algiers* (1955) without first having learned the basics. His cubist work would have been impossible without a firm foundation in realism.

The following concepts are the base on which I build this book. Once we get into it, you'll discover that there is a lot of blending and cross-referencing in acting theory. Frequently, there are two ways to look at the same issue. Before we get into deeper theory and nuance, I'd like for you to keep these basic concepts in mind.

1. *Thinking tends to lead to conclusions; emotion tends to lead to action.* Everything begins with the brain. Human life itself is literally measured in brain activity. A person is declared dead not by the cessation of his heartbeat, but by the flattening of brain waves. Thinking, awareness, and reasoning are fundamental to all humanity. When you walk down the street, it is your brain that keeps you erect and moving, even if you aren't thinking consciously about each step. Zap the brain, and the human collapses. Walt Disney had it right when he observed that "the mind is the pilot." He learned what Aristotle discovered a couple of thousand years earlier. People don't just move, they move for a reason.

"We think of things before the body does them," he explained in a famous memo to the studio's resident art teacher Don Graham (Memo to Don Graham, December 23, 1935). This observation, as self-evident as it may seem now, was revolutionary in animation and led directly to the legendary success of Walt Disney Studios. Beginning with Mickey Mouse, Walt understood that thinking, even if subliminal (a wrestler is moving like crazy, but he's not consciously thinking about moving his arms or legs, right?) leads to movement as well as emotion. Walt gave Mickey a brain! And feelings! He discovered that it is possible to get the audience to *care* about the characters, not just to laugh at them, if the audience thinks the characters have feelings. Disney's characters would be funny, they would have heart, and they would think.

Emotion is a result of the thinking you do with your brain. It can be defined as an *automatic value response* and it happens whether you want it to or not. For animators, it is useful to draw a distinction between thinking and emotion because emotion is what tends to lead to character action. If you want to understand what a character is feeling, it is best to start by asking what the character is thinking and what his value system is.

Thinking tends to lead to conclusions; emotion tends to lead to action

Here's an example: Let's say you are walking alone on a dark street late at night, and you hear footsteps behind you. The thought process works like this: First, you have to determine what the noise behind you actually is. Is it an airplane? A car? A human? Is it a male human or a female human? Is the sound that of footsteps in high heels? Boots? So far, there is no emotion going on. You're just trying to decide what is behind you. Your brain is operating faster than the fastest computer, so you're not really aware of what is happening on a thought-by-thought basis, but it is happening nonetheless.

Ultimately, you determine that the sounds behind you are footsteps of a human and they are getting closer and they sound heavy and insistent. At this point, you begin to experience emotion. If you are a person that has ever had trouble with street crime, or if someone you know was mugged, you will likely feel fear. If, on the other hand, you have been raised in a country or region with very little street crime, like Singapore or China or maybe on a farm in America, then you may not feel fear at all. You may be happy for the company. But for the sake of example, let's say you feel fear. The emotion will tend to cause you to *do* something about it. You might quicken your step, look behind you to see who it is, jump into a doorway, or maybe reach into your pocket for your pepper spray. The emotion is what leads to the action, and the emotion is an automatic value response based on thinking.

When your lover caresses you, you experience emotions based on your personal values, your experience with past lovers, the way you were raised, and the context of the moment. And each person or character is unique. I might feel afraid of heights while you are thrilled at the prospect of parachute jumping. We are all different, but all of us have certain traits in common. We all think, and we all experience emotions. Emotions come from thinking. Walt had it right.

2. *Acting is reacting. Acting is doing.* Bill Tytla (*Snow White*) correctly observed that "the pose is a reaction to something." But it is also true that *all* action is a reaction to something. Your car reacts when you hit the gas; your cat reacts when you step on its tail. You react when your cell phone rings or you get a neck massage. Acting is reacting.

Acting is also *doing*. Acting is both doing and reacting. Your character may be reacting to an internal thought ("I'm thirsty") or an external event such as a fire alarm going off ("Let's get out of here!") or a tasty burger being served up for dinner ("Yum"). The reaction precedes the doing. The traffic light turns red, so what do you *do* about it? You stop the car. You feel a headache coming on, so what do you *do* about

Acting is reacting

it? Take an aspirin. Wile E. Coyote reacts to the fact that Road Runner just foiled him again, and he immediately begins formulating a new plan of attack on the elusive bird. Captain Hook reacts to the tick-tocking of the crocodile by running away. Running away is *doing* something. Note also that each of the examples I'm giving have another component: emotion. First comes emotion, then comes action. First comes a stimulus, then comes action. If you want to show that a character is cold, you first have him react to the temperature—and then he *does* something about it, namely tries to keep warm, perhaps by rubbing his hands together and stamping his feet. How many times have you seen an animated character indicate cold with trembling and chattering teeth? That's weak acting. A person who is cold will *act* to keep warm. The action is in response to the stimulus. Acting is reacting. Acting is doing.

3. Your character needs to have an objective. Theatrical movement is purposeful and significant. Regular ordinary movement lets it all hang out. Any time your character is on stage, you should be able to answer the question, What is he doing? And what he's doing—his action—should be active, in pursuit of an objective. Your character needs to be doing something 100 percent of the time. This kind of *doing* does not mean he is scratching his nose or tying his shoes. Theatrical *doing* is an action in pursuit of an objective. Aristotle referred to this as *unity of action*—small actions that lead to a bigger action, or objective. This simple rule lies at the base of all acting theory. An action without a thought is impossible, and an action without an objective is just a mechanical thing, moving body parts. It isn't theatrical. If your character swats a gnat or moves her lips while she is reading, that is doing something, but it is not in pursuit of a theatrical objective. Movement may be subsidiary movement, shadow movement, and therefore not relevant to her primary objective—or it may be in pursuit of a theatrical objective. When Pluto struggles to get the flypaper off his nose, he is playing an action (get rid of the flypaper) in pursuit of an objective (freedom).

In the movie *Gold Rush*, Charlie Chaplin's Little Tramp wants to impress Georgia, the dance-hall girl, and her friends by hosting them for New Year's Eve dinner. And so he shovels snow to make the money to buy food for a nice dinner. Shoveling the snow and buying the food are *actions*. These actions are in pursuit of an *objective*, namely impressing Georgia. Get it? The objective a character pursues informs the action. If you're trying to figure out what kind of action your character should be playing, or how he should be playing it, ask yourself what the character's objective is.

Acting is playing an action in pursuit of an objective while overcoming an obstacle

5

Suppose for example you've created a scenario in which a character pilots an airplane from Los Angeles to Las Vegas. Getting to Las Vegas is his objective. When he climbs into the cockpit, he'll check the fuel gauge, the brakes, and the controls. His actions have a purpose toward his objective of flying to Las Vegas. Everything else is in support of that. His objective informs his actions. His actions speak of his objectives. And if he's flying to Las Vegas to get married, the *way* he checks the fuel gauge will be affected. If the weather forecast calls for thunderstorms along the flight route, a bystander watching him in the cockpit might notice that he seems nervous. No one would know he is bound for Las Vegas, but they can tell by his energy whether he is just tidying the cockpit, or if he is prepping the plane for a trip. If he has an objective, there will be purposefulness in his movement. And his feeling about his upcoming trip will also affect his body movement. When the Evil Queen is mixing her terrible brew in *Snow White,* her objective is to commit murder. The action she is playing—stirring the pot—is in pursuit of an objective. Take away the intent to kill, and you have a household cook. When the Iron Giant flies off into the sky to detonate the already-launched atomic bomb, flying is his action. Detonation of the bomb is his objective.

4. Your character should play an action until something happens to make him play a different action. Your character should be playing an action 100 percent of the time, even if the scene is purely expository or connective. During one of my Acting for Animators classes in Germany, a student challenged this assertion. "Suppose he's just sitting there?" she asked. "I think it's possible to just sit around, doing nothing." "If someone peeked into this room," I countered, "she could say that you're just sitting around, but the fact is that you have a purpose in being here. You're sitting in a class, learning about acting because it is going to make you a better animator. Maybe one day, you'll run your own animation studio in part due to what you learn here." Then I asked if anybody in the class could come up with an example from a movie in which a character is doing nothing at all.

"*Toy Story!*" said one fellow with a pretty big grin on his face. "When human characters enter the room, the toys stop moving around and become lifeless toys again. They're not doing anything during that time."

I grinned back. "Nope. Good try, though. Actually, the toys are working very hard to pretend they are lifeless. The premise of the movie is that the toys have a secret life. They live! But it's our little secret, so when humans in the story enter the scene, the toys have to put on the old lifeless-toy act."

Your characters should always be doing something, always moving from action to action. To continue with the *Toy Story* example, Woody and Buzz may be squabbling over something, but, when a human enters the room, they pretend to be lifeless. That is a good example of playing an action until something happens to make you play a different one.

Keep in mind that the thing that happens to cause your character to play a different action can be internal as well as external. Yes, a human coming into the room motivates a new action for Woody and Buzz. But suppose Woody suddenly remembered where he left his hat? He would move from one action to another, based on an internal stimulus, namely a memory. It's like when you suddenly remember that you left the stove on, just as you're pulling out of the driveway. The thought will cause you to do something about it, namely to repark the car and return to the kitchen to turn off the stove. You play an action until something happens to make you play a different one.

To further clarify this concept, think of a bead necklace. One bead is next to another is next to another, and so on. String enough beads together and you have a necklace, right? You can't have two beads over here and one bead over there with a big space in between. Constantin Stanislavsky used this image when explaining the necessity to play actions. An amusing side note is that, in the United States, he was misunderstood. Acting teachers in the United States thought he was saying "beats," not "beads." To this

Play an action until something happens to make you play a different action

very day, you will hear acting teachers speak of "beats" in a scene. (Note: A musical beat is a different matter, not to be confused with an acting beat—or "bead.") If you want to really understand what that means, think of beads in a necklace. You can't play an action for a while and then just hang out until another action pops up. Your character needs to be playing an action all the time.

5. All action begins with movement. Breathing is movement. A heartbeat is movement. These movements are so small that the observer can't readily detect them, but they are movements nonetheless. Movement may be imperceptible at first, but there is movement in every action. If you sit quietly and multiply 15×92, there is movement, if only in the shifting of your eyes as you calculate. A thought that is not expressed in action is nothing. An impulse remains an impulse until it is acted upon. When it is acted upon, there is movement. Theatrical action (that is, action that is in pursuit of an objective) usually involves more external movement, that's all. Action without movement is impossible. And remember that movement is a result of thinking.

6. Empathy is the magic key. Audiences empathize with emotion. Empathy means "feeling into." When an audience member empathizes with a character, he relates in a personal way to how the character feels. The importance of empathy in acting is a major theme of

All action begins with movement

this book, and I'll spend more time on the subject later. For now, just remember this: The basic theatrical transaction is between the actor and the audience, and the glue that holds it all together is emotion. Humans empathize with emotion, not with thinking. The audience is why actors act and why you are animating in the first place. The goal of the animator is to expose emotion through the illusion of movement on screen. What the character is doing on a moment-to-moment basis is vitally important, but the points of empathy with the audience involve emotion, how the character *feels* about what he is doing. Empathy is as essential to dynamic acting as oxygen is to water.

7. A scene is a negotiation. A theatrical scene requires an obstacle unless it is a pure connective or expository situation. In the early moments of *The Iron Giant*, Hogarth is riding his bicycle through town to the diner where his mother works so he can talk to her about squirrel ownership. This is a connective scene, getting from one place to another. It doesn't have much conflict in it and that's okay. It sets up the next scene, exposes ambience, and contributes to exposition. The subsequent scene that takes place in the diner is chock full of negotiations and conflict.

In theatrical terms, the word *obstacle* is synonymous with *conflict*. You can simplify the concept by thinking of a scene as a negotiation because negotiations inherently contain conflict.

A scene is a negotiation

Conflict with oneself equals negotiating with oneself

Conflict in a theatrical sense is not necessarily a negative thing. Normally when we hear the word *conflict* we immediately start looking for ways to ease it. Nobody likes conflict. Actors, however, learn that conflict is their friend. There are three kinds of conflict: Your character can have conflict with himself, conflict with the other character in the scene, or conflict with the situation. Put another way, the theatrical moment requires that your character try to overcome an obstacle of some kind. (Television commercials are a different matter. We'll get to that later.) I don't like the word *conflict* much, however, because it sounds negative, like a fistfight in a bar, and conflict in acting is not necessarily a negative thing. You can be in conflict about whether to eat the chocolate cake or the apple pie, about whether to vacation in Aruba or Paris. *Obstacle* is a little better, but it still sounds like something a soldier climbs during basic training. So, instead of those terms, I prefer to take my lead from playwright David Mamet, who refers to scenes as *negotiations*. A negotiation implies conflict, obstacles, opposing needs—but it suggests a search for a positive resolution. You can negotiate with the car salesman, or you can negotiate with yourself about whether to have a second piece of pie. It is always a good idea to ask yourself what is being negotiated in a scene. If you can't find a negotiation, you've probably got theatrical trouble.

The Audience

2

The Actor-Audience Contract

To be an animator, you have to have a sense of the dramatic, a feeling for acting.
—Marc Davis, animator of Cruella De Vil in *101 Dalmatians*

Everything on the stage must be significant. Even if we are playing the most naturalistic play, everything must be done significantly. The actor must have inside him the feeling of significance at all times.
—Michael Chekhov, celebrated 1930s actor and acting teacher

In the two quotes above, Marc Davis and Michael Chekhov are talking about the same thing. This "feeling for acting" or "feeling of significance" is one of the least understood and most important aspects of the actor's art, resting on the premise that actors and audience members have an unspoken but iron-clad "contract" with one another. The basic terms of the contract call for the actor to assume a leadership, high-status position, to take the audience on a journey, to tell a story.

Suspending Disbelief and Animation

The audience, for its part of the theatrical contract, suspends its disbelief in the pretend circumstances on stage. They know the living room walls are actually made out of canvas, that nobody is actually stabbing Julius Caesar, that the actor playing Romeo doesn't really die every night. In effect, the audience presents itself in the theatre and says to the performers on stage, "Take me where you want to. I'm ready to travel!"

Classical animation puts an extra spin on this transaction because it boasts of its nonreality. Animation makes no effort at all to get the audience to suspend its disbelief. Instead, it asks the audience to play along in a more childlike way. Bugs Bunny and Wile E. Coyote are cartoon characters that defy the laws of physics, and there is never a chance that the viewer will think they are real. Donald Duck wears a suit of clothes. Indeed, that's part of the fun. The transaction between animator and audience is more similar to that between children when they play dress-up or tea-and-cake. A little girl who is clomping around in Mom's high heels enjoys the experience all the more because she knows these are Mom's shoes. She has a disincentive to pretend otherwise.

When Tinker Bell almost dies in Disney's *Peter Pan*, the people in the audience do not mutter, "Aw, heck, it's just a bunch of drawings." Instead, they are likely to start yelling at the screen, "I believe! I believe!" in order to save the fairy. They are holding up their end of the contract, you see? When your character performs, you are saying to the audience, in effect: "I (the animator) think these things about this character are important to the telling of this story." The audience's obligation is to suspend its disbelief and play along with you. The audience relates to the characters on screen, but it communicates with you, the animator. In the final analysis, the transaction involves humans communicating with other humans, not humans communicating with drawn images.

This brings us to the special challenges of photo-real animation. With photo-real, we have a whole new set of aesthetic considerations. Take the movie *Final Fantasy: The Spirits Within*, for example. It was sold to the public as the *ne plus ultra* of photo-real. The audience was invited to be amazed at how lifelike was Dr. Aki Ross, the female lead. The movie failed artistically and financially mainly due to story problems, so it never reached the point where it might have stimulated worthwhile discussions about the interface between aesthetics and photo-real. Sooner or later, however, there will be another attempt, and here is the point: Producers of photo-real animation cannot have it both ways. They cannot say to the audience, "This movie is animation and doesn't require suspension of disbelief" while also saying, "This is the animation equivalent of live-action and therefore requires suspension of disbelief." The effort will only confuse and disorient the audience.

It seems to me that most producers of photo-real animation are climbing the mountain just because it is there. Their goal is to create believably lifelike characters that cannot be distinguished from live action. My best guess is that the first producer of a viable and successful photo-real movie will have to sell the story and not the technology. The more that attention is drawn to the technology, the harder it will be for the viewer to enjoy the story. That was part of what went wrong with *Final Fantasy*. (That, plus the fact that the movie had zero humor.)

In the short term, photo-real animation will be useful in video games, which have a different aesthetic standard altogether, and in the depiction of minor background characters in live-action films. Ridley Scott populated the Roman Coliseum with photo-real extras in the movie *Gladiator*. An animated background character in a film can be made to do stunts that are too dangerous or too expensive for live actors to attempt. *Titanic* had all those CG extras falling overboard, for instance. They can be rendered just believably enough not to draw attention to the fact that they are animated because the focus is most often on the foreground characters.

Stage Actors Versus Animators Redux

Actors on stage have the benefit of spontaneous feedback from the audience, and they adjust their performance on a moment-to-moment basis accordingly. The experience of live acting is sort of like riding a wave. The actor is on the surfboard; the audience is the current. That's what makes a theatrical event. But the animator is at a major disadvantage when he enters into this actor-audience contract because he does not receive the immediate feedback from his work that an actor on stage does. Instead, he works alone, playing for the audience in his head, which becomes a surrogate for the intended audience. If you are animating a kid's TV show, you'll make a different kind of performance than you will if you are animating, say, a movie like *Antz*. You do one kind of performance if you are playing for five- to eight-year-old kids and another if you are playing for adults, right? Audiences are not generic, and the audience in your head will take the form of whoever your intended audience is. Broadway actors learn early on that the gray-haired Wednesday matinee audience is a different animal from the more hip audience that shows up on Friday night. The performance varies with the audience. The audience is the cocreator of the show. The animator, then, is sitting in for the audience that isn't there, the audience as he *imagines* it, and he is guessing at its response. (Playwright Jeffrey Sweet writes eloquently about the actor-audience contract as it applies to theatre in his book *The Dramatist's Toolkit: The Craft of the Working Playwright* [1993].)

There is an implied contract between actor and audience

I read a study awhile back in which it was determined that an actor in his first entrance on stage can experience the same blood pressure rise as does a jet aircraft test pilot during takeoff. As an animator, you do not have to personally get up on the stage, but your character does. You get up there vicariously. Because your character acts, and you're the one pulling his strings so to speak, you will experience that adrenaline rush at the first screening of your work. Your character, through you, needs to be thrilled by that same dimming of the house lights that excites actual actors.

Confidence on stage manifests itself in a feeling of *centeredness*, certainty. A good actor—or animator—accepts his position in the pulpit, and feels anchored. That's what the "feeling for acting" Marc Davis speaks of is all about. It's a heightened sense of purpose. The feeling for acting involves knowing that you, through your character, belong on the stage, that you deserve to be there, that you have something worthwhile to say to the audience. It is not enough to merely animate a character, to make him move believably. He must be animated with theatrical intention, theatrical purpose. A moth flying around a lightbulb is animated, but just because there is a lot of wing activity does not make the flight theatrical. Bring in a fly swatter, and you start getting theatre.

Theatrical Reality Versus Regular Reality

The actor-audience contract also requires a certain *kind* of communication. Theatrical reality is not the same thing as regular reality. Regular reality is what you get at the corner grocery store. The theatrical moment—whether on stage or screen, live-action or animated—is interpretative: condensed in time and space, designed for maximum impact on the audience. Animation is not supposed to be "real life." It is more than real life. Regular reality is about letting it all hang out; theatrical reality is about letting *some* of it hang out. Flowers in the garden are lovely, but they aren't art. They become art when Monet or Cézanne paints his impression of them. A pair of old shoes is just a pair of old shoes, but, by the time Van Gogh gets through with his pair of old shoes, we have art. When Charlie Chaplin buys flowers from the blind girl at the beginning

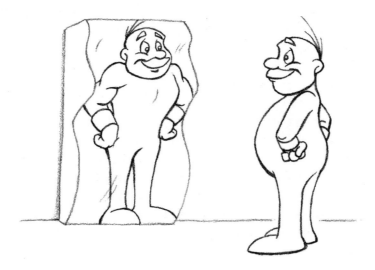

Theatrical reality versus regular reality

of *City Lights*, the moment becomes meaningful beyond the simple reality of the flowers, the girl, or the Little Tramp. Art takes reality to another dimension—one that springs from the artist's brain. The important thing is what Van Gogh *thinks* about his old shoes, what Monet *thinks* about a flower garden, how Chaplin makes a metaphor of the girl's blindness.

Holding the Mirror Up to Nature

Shakespeare said that actors should "hold the mirror up to nature" (Hamlet's advice to the players, Act III, scene 2). What he meant by that is that acting should be a reflection of reality, not reality itself. In order to reflect reality, however, you first have to be acutely aware of it. Hang a camera around your neck; go for a walk through the city streets, and you'll see photographs everywhere you look. Actors have to be like that, but without the camera. Instead of photographs, we are continually taking mental pictures of human behavior. It can be embarrassing for the nonactor companion of an actor when they're out in public because actors will lurk and eavesdrop on even the most personal goings-on. That couple pitching woo in the back booth at the coffee shop deserves their privacy, but their body language is the artist's no-cost classroom—and so he tunes in as the lovers lock eyes, as she leans forward slightly, and his gaze shifts to her bosom. We watch as he, under the cover of a quiet laugh, reaches across the table and places his hand gently on hers. She responds by adjusting her fingers to grip his. That's reality. The spaghetti-eating scene in *Lady and the Tramp* is an artist's reflection of the reality of lovers at a table.

An actor can be in the middle of a heated argument with his partner, things are going hot and heavy, and inside a happy little voice is whispering to his brain: "This is *good*! You can *use* this!" Absolutely everything in life is fair game for the actor. You never know when you can use your memory of, say, the way a particular street person is digging in a trash can. Watch how he retrieves that partially empty raspberry jam jar, checks the label, and evidently decides that he prefers grape or orange marmalade and returns it to the trash. Yep, that's one I've been carrying around with me for twenty years. The old guy was rummaging in a trash can situated at 72nd and Broadway in New York City, and one day I'll use it.

Someone may have observed it earlier, but Aristotle was the first person I know of who pointed out that we humans learn by imitating what we see. Stick your tongue out at a baby, and she'll stick hers out at you. Boys learn how to shave by watching Dad; we all learn the alphabet and arithmetic through a process of imitation. Next time you see a person who is involved in a conversation fold his arms across his chest, notice whether the person he is talking to also does that. Most times, he or she will. We imitate one another a lot. It's part of our human nature. A drawing or an image on celluloid is a representation of real life. We humans experience pleasure in the very act of identifying it as such. When the drawing or image on screen moves and talks, seemingly expressing emotion, we delight in the recognition of our own feelings. Theatrical reality is a copy of reality, which has been highlighted and emphasized in whatever ways the artist deems appropriate in order to communicate his perspective to the audience.

The Character
3

Personality Animation

> The movements and attitudes of a figure should display the state of mind of him who makes them, and in such a way that they cannot mean anything else.
>
> —Leonardo da Vinci

Which is more important: character (personality) or action? Can you have one without the other? Walt Disney was obsessive about personality. Shamus Culhane contends in his books that it is personality first, personality second, and personality third when it comes to animation. Many legendary animators, in fact, refer to the necessity for characters to have colorful personalities—as if personality is something that exists in limbo. Chuck Jones (1989) makes the surprising assertion in *Chuck Amuck* that personality is more important than story. He says, "Personality. That is the key, the drum, the fife. Forget the plot. Can you remember, or care to remember, the plot of any great comedy? Chaplin? Woody Allen? The Marx Brothers?" Well, yes as a matter of fact, I remember the stories of *all* the great comedies, especially those of Chaplin and Woody Allen. How about what is arguably the best comedy of all time, *Some Like it Hot?* It has a marvelous story. I admire Chuck Jones and appreciate what he's getting at, but I think he may be pushing new animators down a dead-end road with this advice about serving a character's personality and not the story. Personality may be the key to something, but what *is* personality? Is it personality if you create a character with a paunch on his belly and one squinty eye? Is character design enough? How does one create personality in a character? Can it be divorced from story? We all understand that Mickey Mouse has a frisky and delightful personality, but what does that mean precisely?

Personality and action are not mutually exclusive. They are not an "either-or" choice. Action defines a character. Donald Duck is a cute character, but if he doesn't *do* something, then he has no personality. Emotions are automatic value responses, and the way a particular character responds emotionally creates the impression of personality. Could you have a dead character with personality? No, of course not. Roy Rogers' horse, Trigger, had a marvelous personality when he was galloping around in those old Republic westerns, but today he stands stuffed in a museum. No personality there except in the memory of people who recall him from the movies.

A thought by itself is just a thought. It's not even a smile. A tendency to blush is a personality trait, but it's not relevant unless the character moves. When you animate a character, you are expressing its thoughts and emotions through the illusion of movement and theatrical action. The movement can be as slight as the tightening of a gaze (Clint Eastwood has made a career of this, in fact) or a Mona Lisa smile, but there must be movement if the character's thoughts are to mean anything to an audience. And the *way* the character's thoughts are expressed amount to its personality. Miss Piggy, my all-time favorite character on *The Muppet Show*, has a strong personality because she is so

Action defines character

self-centered, but her character description won't matter unless she *does* things in a superior manner when she acts. She's the star of her own show in life, and she casts everybody else in the world as supporting players.

Aristotle wrote in the *Poetics* that actions are performed by persons who must have qualities of character and mind. Character and thought, said he, are the two natural causes of action. It is through action that men succeed or fail. We act to live, and we live to act. Walt Disney had the right idea, but Aristotle better understood the process. If you really want to understand acting, study the dynamics of actions first, then the connections between thinking, emotion, and physical action.

Personality in animation began with Disney's *Three Little Pigs* and really came into its own with the seven dwarfs in *Snow White*. True, Winsor McCay's Gertie the Dinosaur had a personality of sorts, but it was primitive compared to the three little pigs. Friz Freleng explains that, in the earliest days of animation, it was enough just to make the characters move—"make 'em walk, make 'em run, make 'em turn around, make 'em talk to each other, in pantomime, of course. But you didn't distinguish one from another; they all did it the same. But when Walt got into distinguishing one from another by personalities, then it changed the whole thing" (Merritt and Kaufman 2000, 81).

Character Analysis

Fred Moore's character and personality analysis of Mickey Mouse, as presented in *The Illusion of Life: Disney Animation* (Thomas and Johnston 1981) goes like this:

> Mickey seems to be the average young boy of no particular age; living in a small town, clean living, fun loving, bashful around girls, polite and as clever as he must be for the particular story. In some pictures he has a touch of Fred Astaire; in others of Charlie Chaplin, and some of Douglas Fairbanks, but in all of these there should be some of the young boy. (551)

That's all, folks. That's the total character analysis of Mickey Mouse.

Fred Moore was, of course, one of the giants of animation, a certified pioneer, and his analysis of Mickey was sufficient for his day. Indeed, he was one of the first to point out that cartoon characters could be made to think. I am not about to criticize Fred

Moore, but the complicated 3-D characters that are being created by animators today cannot get by with such a simple character analysis. Note how almost every reference in Moore's analysis of Mickey is a generality: "no particular age," "average young boy," "a small town," "as clever as he must be for the particular story." *Which* small town? East or west? Probably midwest, similar to Walt's origins, but it wasn't spelled out. What the heck *is* an "average young boy" anyway?

Audience expectations are higher than they used to be when it comes to animation, and an in-depth character analysis is essential whether you are animating a preexisting character or creating a character of your own. Compare Glen Keane's extensive analysis of Ariel (*The Little Mermaid*), to Fred Moore's brief description of Mickey if you want to see firsthand what is happening to animation. Keane, who surely is one of our finest contemporary animators, goes into great depth when describing Ariel. He explains that she is the quirkiest of seven daughters, is sixteen years old, is naive, innocent, and is able to be hurt deeply. He gets into her relationship with her father as well as her relationship with Ursula. In other words, Glen Keane's analysis of Ariel is to Fred Moore's analysis of Mickey what a 747 is to a bi-plane.

You can't just say a character is cute and cuddly and has a great personality, especially if you expect it to carry a lead role in a feature film or television series. Indeed, you can't get away with it even in video games anymore. It makes a difference if the character you're animating is from San Francisco or the Bronx, if he's thirteen instead of sixteen years old, if he likes to play basketball more than he likes to play chess, if he's shy around girls, or if he is deaf in one ear.

And you'll be surprised how character elements that may never be mentioned or used in your animation can still provide strong motivation. For example, the storyline of your script may include no reference to romance, may in fact include no romantic scenes at all, but it is still a good idea for you to know precisely how the characters procreate (here I'm presuming nonhuman characters). If evolutionary theory is correct, and if a species acts to propagate itself, then *all* character activity—even if it is not explicitly about making the beast with two backs—will serve that ultimate objective. In other words, even though you may lay out a very complex and complete character analysis and description, that does not mean you have to make all of those character traits visible.

Let's create a couple of characters together—one human and one nonhuman. Think of a character analysis as a biography. In many animation studios, a "character bible" is maintained for each character in the story. This bible includes a biographical break-down, similar to the following.

Human Character Analysis

Male or female?

Age?

Physical health?

Appearance? Hygiene?

Intelligence?

Diet?

Culture?

History?

Religion?

Income?

Occupation?

Education?

Sexual orientation?

Sense of humor?

Family?

Friends?

Inner rhythm?

Psychology (introvert, extrovert, etc.)?

Goals and dreams?

Name?

Our human character will be a female, seventeen years old, whose name is Jasmine Franco. She is a second-year student at the university in Siena, Italy, and is in excellent physical health, except for occasional stiffness in her left leg, a result of a motor scooter accident four years ago. She is the first child of Gianna and Sergio, and she has a younger brother, Osvaldo, who still lives at home. Jasmine is extremely bright and wants to do everything in life. Sometimes she aspires to be an attorney, other times she wants to be an economist, but, when she is allowing her dreams to take over, what she really, in her heart wants, is to be an archaeologist. Her hobby is history, and she enjoys nothing more than volunteering on historical excavations. Most recently, she participated in a dig in Sicily. Her boyfriend, Paulo, transferred from the university in Siena to one in London at the end of the last school year, which has resulted in very high telephone charges for her parents, who live in Rome, a four-hour drive south of Siena. Jasmine is as graceful as a gazelle, even regal; 5'9" tall, has alert gray blue eyes, thick straw-colored hair, and is extremely popular with her friends. She is multilingual, speaking Italian, French, and English. She projects an outward air of calm and humor, which disguises inner restlessness and a melancholy, poetic streak.

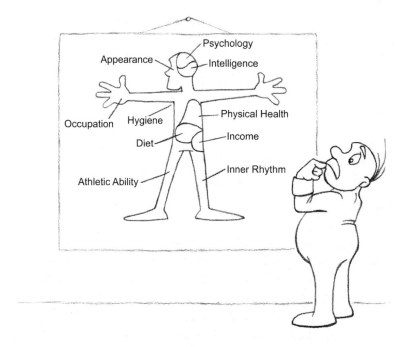

An in-depth character analysis is useful

Now for our nonhuman creature.

Creature Character Analysis

Physical attributes? (Keep in mind evolutionary necessity)

Defense mechanisms/strategies?

Locomotion? (Normal humans walk, snakes slink, Superman flies)

Age?

Life span?

Diet?

Physical health? Physical handicaps? Lost a leg? Hard of hearing?

How does he procreate?

Relatives?

Sense of humor?

Fears?

Goals?

Culture?

Intelligence?

Education?

Relationship to other characters in story?

Source of income? Livelihood? Industry?

Name?

Ferd-Ferd is roughly two hundred human years old but is just a youngster in Sklar time. He's two-and-a-half feet tall when he stands straight up, but of course that is an unnatural posture for him, angling forward as he does. Anyway, when he stands straight up, it causes his receptor eye to dangle uncomfortably. He is bald as are all Sklartons and his soft outer shell is still an adolescent, healthy (and dangerously visible) translucent green. Sklartons don't go to school, but are educated in the irradiating bin while they're in the larval stage. This encodes them with knowledge enough for their early life survival, provides them with a job description, and will successfully sustain most of them when they endure the Predylactus Feast. It's definitely not an easy life being a primary food source for the Predylactus, but Ferd-Ferd nonetheless must make his adult migration to the Elucian Caves in order to mate. Already he is worrying about the upcoming journey, but there is no turning back. Until the dreadful day of departure, Ferd-Ferd will spend his time cultivating life-sustaining Sklar mold back in the rear chamber of the enclave. It's pretty much all work and no play for Sklar youngsters, but Ferd-Ferd and his buddies are always getting into trouble with their pranks.

What the audience sees on stage is just the tip of the iceberg. Eighty percent of what is happening to a character is under the surface, tied up in context, character background, and given circumstances. For example, a man walks into an office, having been summoned by his boss. He brings with him the circumstances of his life, right? Maybe his wife told him just this morning that she is pregnant, or maybe he has been leaving work early for months and is fearful that the boss has finally found out about it. Maybe he has a bunion on his foot, or a headache. All of these things affect what goes on as he enters the office.

Peter Brook, the famous Shakespearean director, gives an important lesson about character and performance animation when he advises that "no matter how much you feel, your character feels more. No matter how much you love, your character loves more."

Primal Analysis

Bugs is simply, and only, trying to remain alive in a world of predators.

—Chuck Jones in *Chuck Amuck*

The theme of life is conflict and pain. Instinctively, all my clowning was based on this.

—Charlie Chaplin

A primal analysis will help you tap in to a commonly shared stream of human values, leading you toward empathic acting choices. It seems self-evident to me that one way or another we humans must get the next generation into being or we will die out as a species. Therefore, when I'm holding that mirror up to nature, I tend to view human behavior as a humongous mating dance, one that is not always graceful. It can be very empowering when an actor finds a strong primal stream for his character. It can sometimes open up a scene or story in unforeseen ways, and it will often explain a character's baffling behavior. At minimum, it can put you in touch with what the character *needs* rather than what he *wants*. A need carries more theatrical voltage and is a more common currency than a want.

For example, in the Tennessee Williams play *A Streetcar Named Desire*, Blanche is in primal competition with her younger, pregnant sister Stella. She struggles throughout the play to appear and behave younger than she is, relying frequently on special effects, the soft flattering light cast by paper lanterns. She tries unsuccessfully—and with increasing desperation—to get local bachelor Mitch to propose to her, but her sexual energy is directed toward Stanley, her sister's husband. Stanley is coarse and simple, a graceful apelike boy/man who possesses extraordinary magnetism. Blanche is high-strung, nervous, painfully aware that her biological clock is ticking, and her old-South, plantation values are in conflict with the modern world. In the end, when Blanche can no longer hide her real age, her dark past or agenda, when she is forced into the harsh light of day she literally implodes, experiencing a nervous breakdown and institutionalization. Before she is escorted to the hospital, however, Blanche and Stanley finally have their sexual day of reckoning.

What draws Blanche to Stanley? We're not talking about teenage passion here, kids tumbling around in the backseat of the Chevy, but something considerably deeper and more complex. Blanche, increasingly unanchored as the story progresses, longs for Stanley's strength, his certainty. It's primal.

The world of animation is full of good examples of primal motivation. Think of Tramp's courtship of Lady in *Lady and the Tramp*, Popeye's love for Olive Oyl, Tarzan's courtship of Jane. The first time we meet the Iron Giant he is trying to find some metal to eat. In classical drama, Anthony literally went to war because of his lust for Cleopatra (*Anthony and Cleopatra*), and Romeo ultimately gave his life for love in *Romeo and Juliet*. When Medea (*Medea* by Euripides), bent on revenge against her husband, Jason, murders her own children as an act of revenge, her crime is almost a dictionary definition of primal motivation. Though she never says it out loud, the Medea principle is that, if you kill a man, you kill him once. But if you kill his children, you kill him repeatedly—

again and again and again, genetically. Medea's man abandoned her, and so she struck back by killing his children. It is no mystery why this story of a woman scorned continues to shock audiences two thousand years after Euripides wrote it.

Two more examples from the world of animation: The Queen in *Snow White* is not merely a vain woman with an "envious heart." She is of a certain age and has an evolutionary interest in being the fairest one in the land. When her magic mirror informs her that she is not the fairest in the land, she obsesses on the demise of lovely, fertile Snow White. It's never made clear who the Queen and Snow White are competing for, manwise—neither in the Grimm's fairy tale nor the Disney movie—but the possibilities are intriguing and perhaps disturbing, given that the Queen is Snow White's stepmother. The most important point, in my view, is that their competition is primal. The Queen is not just *choosing* to destroy Snow White, she's *driven* to do so. She's not a serial killer. The object of her fury is very specific, a young, lovely, child-bearing-age woman. Again, it's primal.

Cruella De Vil has a similar problem with her vanity. Why does she lust for a puppy-skin coat? Surely, it must be because she believes that wearing one will make her more attractive. Even though she is married, a puppy-skin coat will perhaps bring her more attention. One of a kind and all that. Marriage does not stop men and women from wanting to appear attractive to the opposite sex, and this is really the only explanation that makes any sense about Cruella's obsession. The actor's job is to make sense of the character. It's not enough to write off Cruella as an oddball. Oddballs don't think they are oddballs. There must be a reason for a character's behavior, something that drives him, and the more specific the better. In the cases of Cruella and the evil Queen, a primal analysis fits. They are both being pushed along in life, fighting against age, dancing the mating dance, almost like salmon swimming upstream. Neither of them can help themselves.

The justification for a primal analysis is closely related to the mechanisms of empathy. It is not an optional matter that we propagate ourselves. We're wired that way by nature. It is a driving, motivating force behind virtually all human behavior. And, since it is true that humans will respond emotionally to the emotions of other humans, you as an animator are digging in a very rich vein when you find the primal motivation. Most of us don't relate much to the emotions of a sociopath or serial killer because the psychology of such a person is abnormal. But we all do the mating dance, one way or the other, for better or worse, dignified or awkward, and so we all recognize the emotions that the dance brings out in characters on screen. Tex Avery, for one, got a lot of mileage out of this fact of life with his insanely lusting pop-eyed, leering characters.

Evolutionary psychology teaches that "emotions are nature's executioners" (Wright 1994, 88). What that means is that we are hard-wired to feel good about things that are good for propagating our species, like sex. We like sex because it is good for us. And we are hard-wired *not* to like things that are bad for us, like infanticide and incest. Observe that the idea of infanticide—a parent killing his or her own child—causes you to feel more disgusted than the idea of a serial killer. Remember the Susan Smith, child-drowning incident in North Carolina in the early 1990s? She strapped her two young sons into their carseats and pushed the car into a lake. The case created a firestorm of press coverage. I always saw Susan Smith as a Medea figure even though she was portrayed in the press in a different light. The public wanted to string her up for having killed her two children. Internet chat rooms and letters to the editor sections of newspapers were buzzing with calls for her slow torture, preferably by water. Now, compare the public's reaction to another highly publicized criminal, Jeffrey Dahmer. Here was a serial killer that liked to dismember his victims and eat them. Dahmer was the topic of jokes on late-night talk shows, but you never heard a single joke about Susan Smith. Why? Because infanticide is an evolutionary no-no. It's bad for our species. Mothers are not supposed to kill their own children, and the public simply does not find it funny. Nature wires mothers to nurture and care for their children, and, when this goes awry, it is extremely disturbing to most of us. But Dahmer was just a garden variety, sociopathic murderer in the vein of Hannibal Lecter in *Silence of the Lambs*.

All humans act to survive. The first thing we do when we are born is try to live, and the last thing we do before we die is try to live. And we have to propagate ourselves if we are going to continue living for another generation. It is this shared survival mechanism that is at the heart of the empathic response. And remember, as artists we are in pursuit of empathy, not sympathy. When you feel sympathy for someone, you simply feel sorry for him and may or may not empathize. When you feel empathy, you identify with him. A primal analysis leads directly to the empathic response.

The Scene
4

Negotiation

Stanislavsky defined *acting* as "playing an action in pursuit of an objective, while overcoming an obstacle." The word *obstacle* is a synonym for *conflict*. In theatrical terms, this kind of conflict does not have to be negative. A person can be in conflict about whether to eat the blueberry pie or the chocolate cheesecake. This kind of conflict is more like a negotiation. In fact, we can safely say that a scene is a negotiation.

Unless a scene is pure exposition, the kind of thing I call a connective scene, then at least one kind of conflict must be present at all times. (Hogarth's first scene in *The Iron Giant* is exposition. He is riding his bike to the diner where his mom works.) Conflict is essential to drama as well as comedy.

In acting, there are only three possible kinds of conflict:

1. The character can have conflict with another character. "Your money or your life," threatens the thief.

2. The character can have conflict with himself. "I need money, but if I rob this guy, I'm likely to wind up in jail," says the potential thief to himself.

3. The character can have conflict with his situation. "Here is neither bush nor shrub to bear off any weather at all, and another storm is brewing!" cries Trinculo in Shakespeare's *The Tempest*, when he finds himself on a tropical island.

The Fairy Godmother negotiates with Cinderella when she places a midnight curfew on Cinderella's party plans. When Peter Pan saves Tinker Bell's life after she drinks the poison, it is with a negotiation. He asks children everywhere to clap their hands if they believe in fairies. Presumably, if the claps were not forthcoming, it would be curtains for

Your character can have conflict with his situation

Ms. Bell. In *Toy Story*, when Woody agrees to rescue Buzz Lightyear, who has fallen out of the window, the decision involves a negotiation with himself and with the other toys, all of whom are accusing Woody of killing Buzz. When Pluto is struggling to get the fly-paper off his nose, he is in conflict with the situation.

When a scene is giving you trouble, when it feels too shallow, too clownish, when the characters seem to be just making funny faces, stop and look for the negotiation. This can be a marvelously effective litmus test for what is wrong (or right) in a scene.

Status Negotiations

We negotiate status with one another continually, all day long, in all kinds of relationships and interactions. When you go into a restaurant and order a meal, the waiter accords you high status because you are the customer, and he is serving you. There is nothing demeaning about it. This is simply the way the status transaction is playing out

We negotiate status all day long

at that moment. When you are having a simple conversation with a friend, you accord her high status when you allow her to speak; she returns the favor when she listens to you speak. And there are the more blatant kinds of status transactions between parents and their children, husbands and wives, jailers and inmates, between bosses and secretaries. You are reading this book, and, by doing so, you are according me high status, at least for the moment. When a teacher lectures a class, the students are granting her high status. When actors are on stage, the audience is granting them high status.

In order to use this notion of status transactions, you should remove any judgments about it. Status transactions do not usually discriminate, although they could be used that way; they are mainly a way of negotiating interpersonal relationships. Anthony Hopkins used status transactions overtly when he played the butler in the movie *Remains of the Day*. The trick, he said in an interview, was to keep in mind that, from the butler's perspective, all of the space in the room belongs to the master. Whenever Hopkins entered the room, he did so with tacit permission from his master. Observe how a butler helps his master get dressed. He will step into his master's space, presumably by invitation, help him on with his coat—and then step back out! There is a continual acknowledgment on the part of both parties that the master owns the space, and the butler is there to serve. No insults intended. It's a status transaction. Charlie Chaplin used status transactions frequently. When a lower-status character, like the Little Tramp, behaves in a high-status way, maybe putting his feet up on the desk and puffing on a cigar, it is funny. I have achieved remarkable success in workshop scenes by making nothing more than a simple status adjustment. You can do it, too, in your animation. Give one of your characters higher status than the other, and see what happens. The playground bully, for example, is always trying to stake out high status in his dealings with other characters. Kent Manseley, the government agent in *The Iron Giant*, is an adult bully and a coward.

This idea of status transactions is straight out of Keith Johnstone's book titled *Impro*, and I recommend it to you highly. I had been acting for twenty years before I discovered Johnstone. The book is a must-read for all actors and animators.

Scenes Begin in the Middle

Playwrights and screenwriters learn to enter scenes as late as possible. Audiences are smart and can fill in the missing blanks. Indeed, the action will be more fun for the audience if it is allowed to cocreate the scene this way. For example, you don't need to show a character entering the building and then walking up the stairs before he knocks at the apartment door—unless, of course, you want to make a specific point about the climbing of the stairs. Instead, you can begin the scene with the person in the apartment answering the door. Or, you could have the person already in the apartment, and you could pick up the dialogue mid-conversation, maybe with the characters sitting on the sofa in the living room.

Actors operate on a similar principle, namely that a scene does not begin when the lights come up on stage. It begins offstage, where the "moment before" is created. And the scene will not end when the lights fade to black. When an actor is standing in the wings, waiting for his cue to enter, he is connecting with where he (his character) has been, how he came to be standing just outside the entrance to the stage set, and what his intention is when he enters. For example, in the Neil Simon play *Barefoot in the Park*, the newlyweds live on the upper floor of a walk-up brownstone. Whenever the husband enters, he is out of breath from having climbed all those stairs. That is a "moment before." And even more: He may have climbed the stairs wearily or in a head-over-heels hurry, depending on the circumstance, which will also affect the way he enters the scene. Another example: The lights come up on a living room set. A telephone rings. A fellow with a towel around his waist and an annoyed demeanor comes into the living room and answers the telephone. We presume—by filling in the blanks—that he came from the bathroom. If his hair is dripping wet, we presume he got out of the shower to answer the phone. And after he completes his telephone call, exiting in the direction he first entered from, we presume he is returning to the shower. If he exits in another direction, we might presume he is going to the kitchen or something, if we have already been made aware of the apartment floor plan.

Remember: Your character enters a scene with intention, comes from somewhere else, presumably a previous scene and will be continuing on to some other scene after he leaves this one. This ties in with the lesson about playing an action until something happens to make you play a different one. A character should always be doing something.

Here's an another example, this from one of my scene study workshops for stage actors. I was watching two actors present a scene from *The Days of Wine and Roses* by J. P. Miller. The story deals with the ravages of alcoholism, and we were watching the final scene in the play. The husband, now sober, has been in AA for a year. It is midnight and his daughter is asleep in the other room. There is a knock on the door. It is his wife who he has not seen for several months. She enters and explains that she has not had a drink for three days and wants to get back together with him. He refuses because she is still in denial and won't admit that she is an alcoholic. She exits, and that is the end of the play.

After we watched the scene once, it was clear that the actors were hitting all the bases, but, still, the scene was just lying there. It wasn't working. I began to talk to the actors about how scenes begin in the middle.

"What were you doing before your wife knocked on the door?" I asked.

"Well, it's midnight and I'm hanging out."

"Acting theory requires that you be doing something 100 percent of the time. What are you doing? What is your objective?"

He didn't have an answer and so we talked about various things he might do. Finally he decided to balance his check book. I said that was fine, but he needed an obstacle. I suggested that he does not have sufficient funds to pay all the household bills.

"Try to make four dollars turn into six," I instructed.

Then I turned to the actress.

"What is your purpose for entering the scene?"

"I want my husband to take me back."

"What if he has another woman in the apartment with him? Did you think about that?"

No, she had not thought of that.

"How long has it been since you had a drink?" I continued.

"Three days."

"Don't you figure the stress of this meeting would make you really crave a drink? Don't you think that maybe you could use a drink now more than just about anything?"

"Yeah, you're right. I hadn't thought of that."

"One more thing. How long did you stand outside the door before you knocked?"

"Thirty seconds or so."

"Make it five minutes. Try to get your courage up. Try to put on the best face. Try to get yourself ready to make a good impression on him. Then knock."

The actors presented the scene a second time. Now he was balancing his check book and was not waiting for any knocks on the door. The actress was offstage, trying to find courage. She knocked. He looked up and crossed to the door. He opened the door and she walked hesitantly inside, glancing around to see if anybody else was here. She spied one of her daughter's dolls on the sofa and began to weep. The two actors stood there, trying to figure out what to say to one another. Then the scene continued, and it was pure magic.

The adjustment in this case had not to do with the scene itself. It was not about fixing what the audience was seeing. It was about fixing what went on before the scene began. What we did was give the actors actions to play that preceded the scene. When the knock came on the door, the audience was actually watching something now that was already mid-scene.

The Rehearsal

After an actor is cast in a role, he goes into rehearsal. After an animator is cast on a film or television show, he goes into preproduction. For the development of a character and preparation for performance, I think actors have the advantage. Rehearsal is invaluable because the actor usually has the opportunity to work all day long with the director and other actors in the cast, experimenting with various approaches to his role. This process can go on for weeks or even months in the case of a big-budget Broadway show. During rehearsal, the cast is trying to find the beats, rhythm, and tone of the play, the ebb and flow of tension within scenes. An actor may have an idea about how his character should be played, but that can fly right out the window if it doesn't work when put against the reality of what the *other* actors in the cast are doing. Preparing a show for opening night in the theatre is an intense process, the very definition of group collaboration. Everybody knows when opening night is, and rehearsal consists of working things out against the imagined response of the probable opening night audience. This is the rough equivalent of the animator working for that audience in his own head.

A talented director understands that an audience must be touched emotionally if a play is to succeed, so a lot of the rehearsal process is actually devoted to finding those emotional triggers or, as I like to call them, *points of empathy.*

Good animation is also dependent on finding points of empathy, and, even though animators do not enjoy the same sort of free-flowing rehearsal process, I have decided to place a discussion of empathy under the general heading of The Rehearsal. The animator/actor really ought to know this stuff before he can give a solid performance.

Emotion and Empathy

(Those) animators will have to be able to put across a certain sensation or emotion . . . for that is all we are trying to do in animation.

—Bill Tytla, Disney animator, speaking to one
of Don Graham's Action Analysis classes

Our goal . . . is to make the audience feel the emotions of the characters, rather than appreciate them intellectually. We want our viewers not merely to enjoy the situation with a murmured, "Isn't he cu-ute?" but really to feel something of what the character is feeling. If we succeed in this, the audience will now care about the character and about what happens to him, and that is audience involvement. Without it, a cartoon feature will never hold the attention of its viewers.

—Frank Thomas and Ollie Johnston, *The Illusion of Life: Disney Animation*

When we speak of creating *the illusion of life* in animation, it boils down not to manner-isms and naturalistic movement, but to emotion. The audience empathizes with emo-tion. Actors are athletes of the heart. If Pluto gets a sheet of flypaper stuck on his nose (*Playful Pluto*, 1934), the audience laughs because of how Pluto feels about it, his frus-tration as he tries to get it off. Flypaper on a nose is nothing more than an interesting fact if you remove emotion, right? When Pluto only succeeds in shifting the flypaper from one body part to another, he becomes increasingly frustrated; the more excited he gets, the harder he tries to free himself from the flypaper, and the funnier the scene becomes. Emotion builds, laughter builds.

Sociologists and medical and psychiatric experts agree that humans universally express six basic emotions: happiness, surprise, fear, anger, disgust, and sadness. The expression of contempt comes in a close seventh. There is disagreement, however, about whether facial expression is primarily a reflection of inner emotional states or whether it is a social "display." It seems to me that it can be either, depending on the situation.

Thinking that is not expressed as emotion or movement is basically a big zero, a nonevent, mere potential energy. Theatrically speaking, emotion is the goal—that is the essential element of acting, the point of empathy with the audience. When Wile E. Coyote is chasing Road Runner for the umpteenth time, he is driven by emotion. If he stopped to think about it, he'd probably give up the chase because it surely must be clear by now that he is not ever going to catch that bird. We in the audience empathize with his campaign, however, because we have all, at one time or another, been obsessed with something or someone.

Specific—as opposed to universal—situations and emotions are what create a response, a sense of empathy, in your audience. For example, the general fact that all humans die does not produce a feeling of grief in most of us. But the fact that your best friend, Romeo, King Kong, or Bambi's mother has died *does* produce grief. So, if a play-wright or a screenwriter wants to make a statement about the folly of always living for tomorrow, he will create a character that lives that way. When the character faces death and realizes she has missed the sweetness of life by not living fully in the moment, the audience feels her loss and regret. The circuit begins with a general principle, or theme, and works backward to the specific—and the specific moment is the point of contact with the audience. (Whew! And you thought this book was just going to explain why Woody Woodpecker is crazy!) The drama (and comedy) is unique this way, functioning

Empathy is fundamental to human existence

backward from the way, say, most painters work. A painter will paint an image of something specific—a single sunflower, a setting sun, a Mona Lisa—and the viewer forms his own opinion about whatever universal principle may be suggested.

Empathy is not just something we talk about in acting. It is fundamental to human existence. It is evolutionary. Mothers empathize with their babies, which is how they know to pick them up when they cry. If you're standing in the kitchen with your husband when he is cooking dinner, and he slices his finger with a paring knife, you wince along with him because you identify with—empathize with—his emotional reaction to the injury. A psychologically healthy person is an empathic person. A sociopath is notably lacking in the empathy department. If he were empathic, he wouldn't be able to slit someone's throat and then go out for a burger.

President Bill Clinton made a political virtue out of being empathic when he told the voters, "I feel your pain." When King Kong sadly realizes that he can't get out of the cage, the audience empathizes with his feelings of fear and sadness; when the dwarfs cry around Snow White's death bed, we empathize with their grief; when someone wins an Academy Award, the TV-watching audience empathizes with the winner's gleeful feelings. The audience empathizes with emotion, and finding points of empathy is the animator's key to theatrical success.

Paul Ekman and the Expression of Emotion

Since we are talking about organic versus masked emotion, this is a good time to introduce Dr. Paul Ekman. He is a psychologist-researcher-scientist who works out of the University of California, San Francisco, and his field of study is the expression of emotion in the human face. If photo-real animation is an animator's goal, you can be certain that Paul Ekman's well-thumbed books will be lying around the studio. He and his associates have mapped and numbered the muscles (forty-six of them) in the human face and determined that we are capable of making more than 5,000 different and significant facial expressions (1983). Professor Ekman has identified nineteen different versions of the smile, for example. Lovers exchange one kind of smile, and the smile exchanged between customers at the bank is another kind. Also, cultural influences can alter the way that emotions are expressed. European Americans tend to express public emotion differently than Asians, and a child who has been raised in a dysfunctional household will frequently send confusing emotional signals.

Ekman is not an integral part of the animation world at all even though he has lectured at Pixar and DreamWorks, but he's high on the guest list for any photo-real dinner parties. Animators would probably love it if they had a comprehensive encyclopedia of facial expressions they could copy from. "My character is brave but afraid," she might specify while turning to page 346 of the facial encyclopedia to find the appropriate expression. This is pie-in-the-sky stuff because the face is simply too complex and poetic for finite codefying, but Paul Ekman is for sure making a dent in the effort. His latest book, *Emotions Revealed* (2003), includes more than one hundred illustrations of the subtleties of facial expression.

Since the 1960s, Ekman has become a pioneer in the study of facial expressions. He has authored or coauthored a foot-high stack of scholarly papers and books on his subject and lately has begun to attract the attention of the general public. *The New Yorker* magazine ran an extensive article on his work (Gladwell 2002), and *Psychology Today* closely referenced him (Blum 1999). Lawrence Weschler cited Paul Ekman's research in "Coming Face to Face with the Uncanny Valley—Paradoxes of Digital Animation of the Face" in the March 2002 issue of *Wired* magazine. Not to be too grandiose about it, we can safely predict that the study of expression and micro expression of emotion will be increasingly relevant as we humans become more global and anonymous. The expression of emotion in the human face is a tribal thing after all, not a cyber thing. It is important to the way we perceive one another up close in person; the more distant we become from one another, the more essential will be this skill.

Animators have to cherry-pick what they can use from Ekman's research because the larger subject of human expression is bewilderingly complex. He and his associate Wallace Friesen invented the Facial Action Coding System, or FACS, that they are teaching to police departments and terrorism units around the country. What FACS boils down to is a grad course in how to read faces. The police like to use FACS because to understand the minutia of the muscles in the face is to be able to more effectively separate truth from lies when guns are drawn and lives are at stake. Animators would probably like to use FACS, too, except that mastering it involves its own branch of specific

We humans communicate subtlety via our facial expressions

and extensive study. For starters, a person who wants to master FACS has to learn the names for all the muscles in the face. I realize that most animators study physiology and musculature, but Ekman takes this to a whole other second-language level. If you want to lower a character's brow, for example, that involves three separate muscles: the depressor glabellae, depressor supercilli, and the corrugator. If you want to project the emotion of happiness, you must contract the orbicularis oculi and the pars orbitalis in combination with the zygomatic major. Most animators understandably would prefer to animate than to try and master this kind of terminology.

Learning curve aside, animators that work on photo-real animation will have to become increasingly expert at creating the illusion of micro expression because the audience will demand it. The reason is that our human sense of sight is many more times powerful than our sense of hearing. We humans are wired through evolution to communicate subtlety via our facial expressions. Though the average person on the street may not be able to enunciate this reality, it is nonetheless how he will function in his interpersonal relationships. If you show him photo-real animation on the screen, he either will or will not respond organically. Animators who are working on the next generation of photo-real will, therefore, necessarily have to come to terms with precisely the kinds of things Ekman is talking about.

Charlie Chaplin and Empathy

Walt was really influenced by Chaplin. He thought of Mickey Mouse actually as a little Chaplin. Walt kept the feeling of this droll, kind of pathetic little character who was always being picked on but cleverly coming out on top anyway.

—Dick Huemer, Disney storyman

I thought of the Tramp as a sort of Pierrot. With this conception I was freer to express and embellish the comedy with touches of sentiment.

—Charlie Chaplin

I admired Chaplin very much because you could see him think, and plan, and you cared for him.

—Chuck Jones

> Even funnier than the man who has been made ridiculous is the man who, having had something funny happen to him, refuses to admit that anything out of the way has happened, and attempts to maintain his dignity.
>
> —Charlie Chaplin

> All great cartoon characters are based on human behavior we recognize in ourselves.
>
> —Chuck Jones in *Chuck Amuck*

Charlie Chaplin brought empathy to comedy. His brilliance and innovation as a performer made him the first international movie star and his influence on the world of comics and animation is huge. Cartoonist Pat Sullivan, for example, borrowed from Chaplin when he was drawing the *Sammy Johnsin* comic strip back in 1917. And later Sullivan and Otto Messmer produced a Little Tramp comic strip that was wildly popular. When Messmer moved from comic strips to animated films, many people considered his Felix the Cat character to be a knock-off of Charlie Chaplin.

But it was Walt Disney who got the most mileage out of Chaplin. He and Disney's resident art teacher Don Graham made sure that the Disney animators at the old Hyperion Boulevard studios in Los Angeles studied Chaplin movies frame by frame. Graham and the animators would do "action analysis" on them, studying the dynamics of Chaplin's movement and watching how he set up his gags. To be sure, they also studied Buster Keaton, Laurel and Hardy, and the other silent film stars, too, but it was Chaplin who was the most influential by a good distance.

What made this little man so popular and important? Some folks argue that it was his funny walk, the big shoes, the cane he twirled, his mustache. Yes, all of those things are funny, and they may have contributed to Chaplin as an endearing personality, but it was his ability to inspire empathy that was his true genius. Chaplin understood how to play to the heart, how to evoke laughter one moment and tears the next. Since he was targeting an international audience in a time before the talkies, he continually searched for the things that all humans have in common, the things that make us laugh and cry. Chaplin understood that audiences empathize with feelings, not thoughts or gags, and he looked for ways to allow the feelings of the Little Tramp to be visible. The important thing was not what happened to the Tramp, but how he *felt* about what had happened to him.

Empathy and *sympathy* are not interchangeable nouns. Psychologist Edward Tichener coined the word *empathy* in the early 1920s. It is derived from a German word, *Einfühlung,* which literally means "feeling into." The German word had been brought into use around 1907 by art critic Theodore Lipps because he was searching for a way to describe a mode of aesthetic perception. A person could "feel into" a painting, for instance. *Sympathy,* which means "feeling for," does not capture the same meaning as *empathy.* If you feel pity or concern for another person, that's *sympathy.* Empathy means that you identify with, and share in, the other person's feelings.

If an audience merely feels sorry for the character, the scene will fall flat. When a viewer empathizes with the character on screen, he is seeing in himself the potential to behave like that character is behaving. In a word, he *identifies* with the character. Empathy is based on the fact that we all act to survive, to live. Doesn't matter which culture or country, we start breathing at birth, and we keep trying to breathe until the last moment of our lives. Sounds simplistic, but it is actually a very profound truth for animators to recognize. In order for acting to rise to the level of art, it must inspire empathy. (Bertholt Brecht's theories respectfully excepted because they are not relevant to animation.) This was the difference between Sennett's Keystone Cops and Chaplin's work as the Little Tramp in *The Gold Rush.* In the Keystone Kops series, there was no script, no plot to speak of, and the gags involved chase scenes and prat falls. Pure slapstick comedy. A Kop would get his foot caught in a bucket and try to shake it off, kicking around wildly. That was the kind of comedy that was popular when Charlie Chaplin arrived in America. When the Little Tramp got his foot caught in the same bucket, he too tried to shake it off—but he would look around to see if anybody noticed his predicament. He was embarrassed by it. Immediately, the audience would empathize because we have all gotten our foot caught in the figurative bucket at one time or another. When the Keystone Kops did it, the audience laughed *at* the Kop; when Charlie did it, they laughed *with* him.

I'll wager that you have had many Chaplinesque moments in your life and didn't even realize it. I'll tell you about a couple of mine. When I first moved to sunny Los Angeles from chilly New York in 1976, I decided to go to the beach. Parking being a big problem in Santa Monica, I drove north along the Coast Highway until I found a grocery store with a large parking lot on the east side of the Coast Highway. Leaving my car in the lot, I made my way in a westerly direction, climbing through the broken chain link fence. I walked along a winding out-of-the-way foot path that doubled me back under the highway and deposited me onto a small and lovely beach not too far north of the ultra-rich Malibu Colony. After laying out my blanket on the sand, setting the portable radio dial to the golden-oldies station, and lathering on the suntan lotion, I glanced around at the people on the beach, pleased with myself for having settled in like a local. That was when I noticed the two of them, a handsome young man and woman, just emerging from the ocean, stark naked. Focusing more closely, I shifted my view slightly to my right to see if anybody else noticed Venus and Adonis. Several more bare bottoms shone in the sunshine. I looked to my left, same thing. Then it dawned on me that some of the folks were starting to look at *me* with annoyed expressions on their faces! I casually checked my watch, considered for a moment the nonexistent appointment I had forgotten about, gathered my blanket and accouterments and, as if I passed this way every Sunday, walked slowly back to the path that had led me to what was obviously a clothing-optional beach. On the way back to the car, I imagined the scene I had just been part of as it might have been played in a comedy movie. The actor playing my part would have gawked at the nudity, his jaw dropping with incredulity. But that would have been cheap movie-making. In real life, I had personified a Chaplin moment. My first impulse was not to gawk (though I surely was gawking inside), but to look around to see if anybody else realized there were naked people on the beach. In other words, I didn't play the moment for laughs, but for the humanity, which made it really funny.

Charlie Chaplin's Little Tramp character was just that, a tramp, a drifter. Chuck Jones says he knows of no lasting comedian who was not a loser, and he cites Chaplin as an example. I understand his point because the Tramp rarely had more than a few coins in his pocket, and he was never very far from starving, but I disagree about the loser part. There is a major difference between being a victim and being victimized. The Little Tramp was no victim. He was a survivor who was frequently victimized. No matter how dismal the circumstances of his life were, no matter how hungry or cold he was, he never gave up, and he never lost his self-respect. There was pathos to the Little Tramp, yet he did not want to be pitied. If he had given up, if he indeed were a loser, the unspoken audience reaction would be, in effect, "That Little Tramp sure is a sad character. I hope he can get his act together. I, on the other hand, would never give up." In other words, the audience would *sympathize* with the Little Tramp, but if he gave up the good fight, they would not *empathize*. This is, in my opinion, one of the major differences between the comedy of Buster Keaton and that of Charlie Chaplin. Keaton frequently drew sympathy with his expressionless reactions and hangdog demeanor. In a BBC television documentary about his life and achievements, Keaton said that he never *tried* to make audiences feel sorry for him, but "if they did, that was okay." I am convinced that this is the reason Keaton occupies a slightly lesser seat in cinematic history than Chaplin does. He was a brilliant clown and mime, but he was uneducated and unsophisticated about the actor/audience contract and empathy. Walt Disney had an innate understanding of empathy, which was why I think he identified with Chaplin so much.

Charlie Chaplin never used the actual word *empathy*, but he had a solid grasp of the empathic process. He just knew. He was brilliant. In *The Adventurer*, for example, he included a gag in which he spilled an ice cream cone down the dress of this upper-class matron. Explaining the psychology behind the gag some years later, he said,

> There were two real points of human nature involved in it. One was the delight the average person takes in seeing wealth and luxury in trouble. (It would not have been funny for the ice cream to have fallen on a poor woman.) The other was the tendency of the human being to experience within himself the emotions he sees on the stage or screen. (Robinson 1985, 202)

That's empathy.

One of my personal favorite on-screen examples of Chaplin's sense of empathy is in *Gold Rush*. When it becomes clear that Georgia the dance-hall girl is standing up the Little Tramp, that she will not come to dinner in the cabin, he is crestfallen. As strains of "Auld Lang Syne" waft from the bar downtown to the cabin, the Little Tramp knows that Georgia is not coming. In that moment, when Charlie is standing in the open door of that cabin listening to the distant music, he is the saddest man in the world. And this moment happens in a comedy! We in the audience empathize with that. We feel his sadness; we all know what it feels like to be stood up. This is Chaplin's genius, and it is a great acting lesson for all actors and animators. Go for the empathy as much as the gag. Remember the heart. Don't just try to be funny. Evoke tears as well as laughter.

All of acting rests on the search for the positive motivation, the survival mechanism, in the characters. As Walter Kerr once observed, "The secret of Chaplin, as a character, is that he can be anyone" (1990 [1975], cover). No matter what the awful circumstance, Chaplin's character always hung on to a basic respect for the human race. He was serious and funny, both at the same time. "All of my pictures are built around the idea of getting me into trouble and so giving me the chance to be desperately serious in my attempt to appear as a normal little gentleman," he wrote early in his Hollywood career, adding: "That is why, no matter how desperate the predicament is, I am always very much in earnest about clutching my cane, straightening my derby hat, and fixing my tie, even though I have just landed on my head."

Now, apply the empathy litmus test to your favorite cartoon characters like, say, Bugs Bunny or Sylvester the Cat and see if they are not cock-eyed optimists, too. Chuck Jones acknowledges that Bugs' optimism is a key element in the rabbit's character, and I'm surprised he didn't recognize Bugs' roots in Charlie Chaplin's work. As the old saying goes, "Everybody loves a winner." It started with Chaplin. Pop some corn, put your feet up, and study him hard.

Acting Is a Process of Exposing, Not Hiding

This is another of those tricky distinctions between actors and animators: When creating a character, an actor tends to work from the inside out; animators, by contrast, tend to work from the outside in. Actors think of exposing themselves through the character. When acting is right, it feels mildly embarrassing, like you are taking off your clothes in front of strangers. The animator doesn't work like that because he doesn't work in the fleeting moment. But this is important: The fact that actors expose themselves is what makes each actor's perspective unique.

While it is true that the audience sees a finished and well-developed character on stage when the curtain goes up, the actor who created the character does not experience the process of acting as hiding, or becoming another person. To him, it feels like truth telling. From an actor's perspective, the goal is to merge his own honest impulses with those of the character he is playing. I'm not suggesting that the actor tries to make each of his characters behave like the actor does in real life. No, the challenge for the actor is to identify what the character is doing in the scene, and then to find in himself the impulse that will lead to that action.

Acting is a process of exposing

Actors do not become the characters they play. You can't, in reality, be anybody other than yourself, right? You can't be me, and I can't be you, and neither one of us can be Hamlet. But we both understand vengeance in our own ways, and therein lies the secret of how you and I can both play Hamlet. Our performances would be similar in that we both say Shakespeare's lines, but what you think makes Hamlet tick is different from what I think makes Hamlet tick. We each look at life in our own unique way.

The fun in acting is to play characters that are different from yourself because, when you do, you are telling an audience what it is that you understand about this character. This is how acting rises above the Mickey Rooney, "Hey, kids, let's put on a show!" level and becomes art. At its artistic best, all acting is character acting. But we don't so much "create" the character as we "release" the character. Michelangelo spoke of exposing the hidden figure within the marble rather than creating a figure. So it is with actors and their characters.

We have the potential to be anything in life. If you had been born into less money or more money, or if you had lost a foot in a motorcycle accident when you were sixteen, your life would be quite different today. If your mother had died in childbirth, you'll never know how her influence on you might have affected your ultimate maturity. Given your genetic parameters, circumstances in your life are what mold you. It is possible that, given different circumstances in your life, you might have turned out to be an U.S. Senator, a doctor, or a clown at Ringling Brothers. You could be in jail or in a monastery or on the moon, given different circumstances in your life.

In life, we emphasize the character traits that get us the most mileage, the most success. One person's demeanor may be that of the jokester, another takes the quiet, studious approach. Yet another is a born politician. There is a good chance that the quiet studious person got that way partly because nobody ever laughed at her jokes much anyway. The jokester, by contrast, gets plenty of positive feedback for his gregarious ways. When you are acting, you find the parts in yourself that would be like the character you are playing, and you hoist those up the flagpole, allowing them to be more powerful than your regular street personality.

When an actor is cast in a role, he does not spend a single moment denying that he could himself turn out to be like the character. If he were going to play a murderer, he would not deny in himself the potential for murder. Instead, he would study the play, learn about the character, and try to find points of empathy, conjunction between himself and that character. If he were cast to play Stanley Kowalski in *Streetcar Named Desire*, for example, he would try to find the part of himself that expresses himself physically. Stanley is not a man who is good with words. In a moment of frustration, he is more likely to wipe the dishes off the table, sending them flying into the wall, than he is to talk things out in the family counselor's office.

Adrenaline Moments

Definition: An adrenaline moment is a moment that the character will remember when he or she turns eighty-five and looks back on his life. It is, in short, a moment of significance.

Have you ever noticed that you tend to remember particular moments in your life more than others? You will always remember the first time you made love, for example, but you will have trouble remembering what you had for breakfast the day before yesterday. You will remember everything about what you were doing on 9/11. You will remember the day you met your spouse. You will remember the day your first child was born.

Scientists have discovered that when something important (i.e., important to our survival as humans) happens to a person, her brain literally becomes bathed with adrenaline. Nature marks this moment and instructs that she remember it. The moment may be happy or sad, full of excitement or very quiet. None of that matters. All that matters is that the moment be important. The time you saw your friend get eaten by a saber-tooth tiger, your brain was bathed with adrenaline and marked. That way, you would respond with fear the next time you saw one of those animals approaching. It is a survival mechanism.

I have extended this physiological concept into storytelling and acting. I am convinced that effective storytelling necessarily includes at least one adrenaline moment, and it may include many. *The Iron Giant* is chock full of these moments, for instance. Darn near every scene is so important that the characters involved will remember it when they turn eighty-five. Hogarth will always remember the day he first met the Giant. Dean will always remember the day that Hogarth's squirrel ran up his pant leg

An adrenaline moment!

in the diner. Everybody on earth will remember the day the Giant chose to fly into space to intercept the bomb.

An adrenaline moment doesn't have to be a big earth-shaking deal. In the famous Disney animation of Pluto getting the flypaper stuck on his nose, that is an adrenaline moment for Pluto. It works theatrically because it is important to the dog and because the scene involves actions, obstacles, and objectives. The world will not change because of the flypaper. The moment is comparatively insignificant when compared with world wars and such, but it is important to the dog, and that is all that matters. Pluto will never forget his encounter with the flypaper.

I saw an advertisement the other day for a bird-feeding contraption that will literally fling hungry squirrels off into the bushes. It is battery operated and is hysterically funny to look at. Squirrel climbs up to get some food and the whole thing starts spinning, with the squirrel hanging on for dear life. Well, we have the makings there of an adrenaline moment for the squirrel, if anybody decides to make an animation out of it. For sure, the hapless squirrel will not forget the day he encountered the squirrel-flipper bird feeder.

An adrenaline moment is a factor of character. It is not a factor of story. The story per se does not have an adrenaline moment because the story's brain doesn't get bathed in adrenaline. The *character's* brain gets bathed with adrenaline. An adrenaline moment is also not something that happens to the audience. The audience does not experience an adrenaline moment unless the theatre burns down while the movie is screening. The person in the audience *empathizes* with the character that is experiencing an adrenaline moment.

In my Acting for Animators classes, I like to show Michael Dudok de Wit's award-winning short animation "Father and Daughter." The story is about a young girl spending her life coming to terms with her father's death. The single adrenaline moment in the piece is the day the father dies. The movie has no other such moment, but that single moment powers the whole thing.

How to Use the Adrenaline Moment Concept

You can super-charge a scene if you make it into an adrenaline moment. Clearly, you don't want to do this for every single scene in a story. If a character is threading a needle, for instance, that may very well not be an adrenaline moment. It would become one if, say, the needle got embedded in the person's finger and he had to go to the doctor to get it taken out. You would not want to arbitrarily make an adrenaline moment out of an average scene. But if you have a story that seems not to have *any* adrenaline moments in it, you may well want to reassess the significance of your story. Why are you telling the story in the first place? What is important about it? Why does it matter?

If you are making your own animation, ask yourself if the story you are telling is worth calling the tribe together. Actors are shamans, and so are animators. When you tell a story, there needs to be some point to it. If you call the tribe to assemble, be sure that you have something worthwhile to say.

If you are assigned a scene to animate on the job, ask yourself if it is possible that this is an adrenaline moment for one of the characters. Check with the director. In my stage-acting classes, I will sometimes suggest to actors that they play an energyless scene a second time, making it into an adrenaline moment. What this means is that they should make the scene important enough that the characters will remember it when they turn eighty-five. Most often, this is a very constructive adjustment.

Heroes and Villains

> The queen in *Snow White* had to be cold, ruthless, mean, and dramatic. Nothing would be gained by developing her personality any further or by letting the audience discover her weaknesses. Like a Shakespearean monarch, she had to be regal and beyond the reach of common people.
> —Frank Thomas and Ollie Johnston in *The Illusion of Life: Disney Animation*

Frank Thomas and Ollie Johnston speak at length about the making of Disney villains in their book named, appropriately enough, *The Disney Villain* (1993). They are explicit in their insistence that the villain must be bigger than life and have no regrets. It seems to me that this might be a workable formula for a classic fairy tale, which is what their masterpiece *Snow White and the Seven Dwarfs* is, but animation today is sailing past the fairy-tale stage, taking its place in the mainstream of adult entertainment. Fairy tales don't traffic in subtleties. They require an archetype hero and villain, a moral conclusion, and that's enough. When it comes to the heroes and villains of the twenty-first century, however, we need to create more nuanced characters.

Avoid one-dimensional villains

Consider for a moment the Disney animated version of *The Hunchback of Notre Dame*. It appears to me that the story's villain, Claude Frollo, was created in the mode of the queen in *Snow White*—a one-dimensional baddie—and I'm guessing this is a formula that can be traced back to the reasoning of the Nine Old Men. Frollo is, in my opinion, dastardly from first entrance to final exit, the kind of character that would kick babies down the stairs. Following the logic from the 1930s and 1940s, I can see where the creators figured this would be frightening—but Victor Hugo's *The Hunchback of Notre Dame* is decidedly not a fairy tale. It would not have taken much to flesh out Claude Frollo's character a bit, and I contend it would have made for a better movie. I'll get back to this scenario and my rationale in a moment, but first let's try to come up with workable definitions of *hero* and *villain*.

To me, a hero is an ordinary person who has to rise to extraordinary heights to fight an extra-extraordinary villain or situation. Alfred Hitchcock made a hero out of Cary

Grant in *North by Northwest*. Gary Cooper was certainly a hero in *High Noon*, a workaday sheriff who has to defend an entire town single-handedly. Jimmy Stewart was a hero in *Mr. Smith Goes to Washington*, fighting political corruption, the biggest and ugliest enemy of all. A passerby who pulls victims out of a burning car wreck is a hero. A parent who jumps in front of a car to protect his own child is not. A naturally talented athlete is not a hero, even if he climbs Mount Everest, but an athlete who overcomes a diagnosis of terminal cancer to win the Tour de France, as Lance Armstrong did in 1999, is a hero in my book. Those few who smuggled Jews out of Germany during WWII were heroes, but an Army general is not a hero just because he is a general. And, yes, Quasimodo—hunchback, bad eye, and all—would fit my definition of a hero. Despite his unusual abode in the cathedral, and the cruel circumstances of his upbringing, he is basically an ordinary kind of person who longs to be just one of the gang.

A villain, by contrast, is an ordinary person who has a fatal flaw, a blind spot in his psychology, something that torments him and causes obsession. Captain Nemo in *20,000 Leagues Under the Sea* is a great villain. Adolph Hitler was a villain. Captain Ahab in *Moby Dick* is a great villain. One of my favorite cinematic villains is Cruella De Vil in *101 Dalmations*. She's a regular enough lady, but she has this flaw that causes her to obsess about owning a puppy-skin coat. Hannibal Lecter in *Silence of the Lambs* and its sequel is the very definition of an excellent movie villain—a medical doctor run amuck, morphed into a serial killer who—gasp!—cannibalizes his victims! You don't get much more awful than that, now do you?

Okay, now that we know what heroes and villains are, let's talk about what to do with them acting-wise. The key once again, still and always, is empathy.

An actor's job is to create in the audience a sense of empathy, and this is true whether the character is a hero or a villain. If I were cast to portray Hitler, I would try to find in myself the potential to do what he did. Hitler didn't think he was evil or a villain. He figured the world had a Jewish problem and needed what Germany had to offer as a solution. As ugly as that may be, I—as an actor—must justify such behavior. It does me no good at all to deny that I have the potential to carry out mass executions. If, after my performance as Hitler, members of the audience say to themselves, "My God, I understand the man! I can see how this terrible thing happened and might could happen again!" then I am a success. If they say on the way out, "Yep, that Hitler was an evil fellow okay. Good thing he's dead, God and the U.S.A. prevailed, and we don't have to worry about people like him any more,"then I have failed. The point of art is to say something about life, about living. It's not about preaching to the choir.

Whenever I hear an actor in one of my classes say that she cannot relate to the character she is playing, I stop the class cold. It is virtually impossible to give a compelling performance if you cannot relate to your character, if you do not in fact *like* your character.

When Anthony Hopkins portrayed Hannibal Lector, he had people in the audience actually rooting for the cannibal. You know why? Go back and watch the movie again and you'll see that Hopkins allowed in these little slivers of humanity. In the scene where Jodi Foster stands outside his cage and tells him about how her father met his violent death, you can see in Hopkins's nonverbal reactions that he is (1) stimulated by her description of death and (2) empathizing with her feelings of loss. It's the second part that makes Hopkins's work so wonderful. He makes us identify with the man. We all can identify with the emotions of a person who has lost a loved one. Brilliant acting.

Now let's return to Frollo's character development. There is a lot to admire about Disney's version of *The Hunchback of Notre Dame*, not least of which are the gorgeous Paris backgrounds and the catchy show tunes. And it was to be expected that Disney would convert pathetic, stone-deaf, silently furious Quasimodo into a sort of good-natured chipmunk of a fellow with a back problem and one cute eye. But a fundamental error was made in the adaptation of the villain, Claude Frollo from novel to animation screen. This factor, more than any other, robs the movie of the greatness it might have otherwise achieved. In this movie, we just don't get to feel the humanity in Frollo. We never even hear about how he cared for his younger brother after their parents died, or why he was moved to protect and raise Quasimodo in the first place. Indeed, in the movie, his first reaction to the idea of adopting the child is to protest. "What?! I'm to be saddled with this misshapen . . ."

From beginning to end, the animated Frollo is unempathic. There is no way for an audience to identify with him—and he therefore loses some of his power to frighten. The thing that is scariest is the recognition of the villain in each of us.

It would not have taken much to do for Frollo what Hopkins did for Hannibal Lecter. A single scene in which he could experience amusement, a touch of human kindness, would have done the trick. Those figurines that Quasimodo carved in his living quarters presented an opportunity. It appears that the only reason for them to be in the movie was to set up the commercial tie-ins. But suppose Quasimodo was carving the delicate figures to please Frollo? Suppose Frollo was truly charmed by them? A moment of gentleness perhaps? Suppose Frollo were charmed and then, as a reaction against his own weakness, he swept the figurines off onto the floor! That would have created a point of empathy. A warm connection between Frollo and Quasimodo, however fleeting, would have made the later terror in the movie much more frightening. Heck, it would have been nice if Frollo had even liked his horse! When he tumbles from the cathedral at the end of the movie, we are supposed to be happy that there are no more Claude Frollos among us. The one who existed has bitten the dust. To me, that is not getting the most mileage for the villainous buck.

It is true that, in order to have a strong hero, you have to have an even stronger villain. The stakes have to be huge in order to make the fight worthwhile in cinematic and theatrical terms—and to carry a theme.

If *Snow White and the Seven Dwarfs* were farce, I would agree with Thomas and Johnston when they say that there would have been no gain in deepening the character of the queen. Maybe they're right, and we'll never know for sure, but in general I contend that you cannot go wrong by making your villains empathic. True, it is frightening to have a big train boring down on you, but it is more frightening to know that a sociopath is at the controls.

Movement
5

Animation is movement. Movement is animation. What a person in the audience sees creates a much stronger impression than what he hears. In fact, if you want to prioritize the senses, they would rank this way:

1. Sight: We see something before we can hear it.
2. Hearing: We hear something before we can smell it.
3. Smell: We smell something before we can touch it.
4. Touch: We touch something before we can taste it.
5. Taste: Taste is intimate, as close as we can get.

A character's body language is going to transmit a more powerful message than his dialogue. Politicians and Madison Avenue ad execs understand this better than anybody, which explains all those flag-waving, sappy campaign ads that saturate the airwaves every couple of years. It doesn't really matter what sort of awful lies they are telling, just as long as they're kissing babies and standing in front of a flag. Anthropologist Edward T. Hall says in his book *The Hidden Dimension*, "it is probable that the eyes may be as much as a thousand times as effective as the ears in sweeping up information" (1969, 42). The evolutionary reason for this is that when we were still running around on the savannas, hiding from saber-toothed tigers, we had to be able to detect predators before they were close enough to eat us. If we had to wait until we could hear or smell them, we'd be lunch.

For proof of the power of visuals, consider how long it takes for you to form an impression about the people that you see on the street. I am writing this paragraph while sitting in the window of my favorite Italian coffee shop in downtown Palo Alto,

Visuals lead to conclusions about your character

California, on a sunny October afternoon. A steady stream of cars and pedestrians is passing by on University Avenue outside, but street noise is isolated from me. All I can hear is the music on the store music system and the happy chatter of a few patrons. The fact that I can't hear outside noises, however, doesn't stop me from forming conclusions about what I am seeing. There is a man sitting directly across the street from me, for example. He is under a tree in front of the bank; he has freshly barbered blonde hair, is beardless and is in a wheelchair; he just finished drinking what appears to be a milkshake or soda from a large Dixie cup. He is lighting his cigarette with a lighter, not a match; he is wearing a loose-fitting burgundy T-shirt and black slacks; his left foot is propped up on the frame of the well-traveled chair, causing his left knee to jut higher above his lap than his right. That suggests to me that he is not paralyzed from the waist down. He may be thirty years old and appears to be in good general health except for not being able to walk. He looks brighter than the average bear, probably has at least a high school education and, this being mid-afternoon on a weekday, is probably unemployed. The fact that he lit his cigarette with a lighter says to me that he is a regular smoker and may have an obstinate attitude. Everybody knows smoking is a health hazard, so why would a person who is already in a wheelchair be smoking? I figure he probably is the sort who will not let anybody tell him what to do. Smoking is a signal of his independence.

Now the truth is that I have no basis on which to conclude these things about that man. I don't know why he is in that wheelchair or, in fact, anything at all about him. It is unfair for me to be forming any conclusions, yet I do it. You, too, form continual and immediate impressions based on what you see—and more relevant to the topic under discussion, so does every member of every theatre and movie audience in the world. The visual impression created on stage or screen is more important than the spoken word. This is why I am firmly convinced that strong animation can save a weak voice-actor performance, but the strongest voice performance cannot save weak animation. (I'm frequently annoyed by reviews of animated features because too many reviewers credit the voice-actors with the success of the final film, treating the animation almost as an incidental element!)

Of course, I'm not suggesting that visuals and sound are an either/or proposition. Both music and sound effects accompany movies. The music frequently creates a mood that vastly enhances the visuals. The Gary Cooper movie *High Noon* is a good example. In it's pre-release edited form, the haunting theme song, "Do Not Forsake Me, Oh My Darlin'" was not included. Studio execs decided the movie didn't work and insisted that the track be added. I defy you to imagine that movie without the song. It makes the movie!

This fact of life about vision versus hearing is an appropriate introduction to the general topic of movement. Movement does not exist in a vacuum. Your arms, and the dog's legs, don't just flail around senselessly. Movement is usually a result of thinking and emotion. An animator really should have a profound understanding of the connections between thoughts and movement, emotion and movement, how movement impacts the audience, and how it impacts other actors in the scene.

Animating Force Versus Form

Recently, I was rereading a transcript of a Don Graham class at the old Disney Studio. His subject was the importance of animating force rather than animating mere forms.

He rightly pointed out that if you draw the form of a leg and then another bunch of forms of legs, it might all flow together as a moving image, but it will not stimulate the audience emotionally. To have that effect on an audience, he explained, you must animate force. And force is most often something that originates in the character's thinking and emotion.

The bookends of human life are brain waves, that is, thinking. Medical science can keep hearts and bodies alive mechanically now, but when the brain stops, that's the end of the party. This is more than a simple observation. It is a profound connection between all humans, something that we all have in common. It doesn't matter if we are talking about Mother Teresa, Osama Bin Laden, or Tom Cruise, we all come into the world the same way, and we exit the same way. We are all part of the same family. While we may disagree with one another about the best ways to spend our time between entrances and exits, we are hard-wired by nature to recognize in one another the very *attempt* to spend the time. And that *attempt* manifests itself as the force that Graham was talking about. To paraphrase Gertrude Stein, a body is just a body is just a body, even if it is an inert one. The thing that causes us to pay attention to one another as humans is force—the way we go about living and spending the time. Acting is *doing!*

Though all of us humans have thinking brains—making us all part of the same family—the *kind* of thinking we do varies from person to person. Because each of us is an individual product of our genes and environment (nature vs. nurture) the key to successful character animation is understanding the character's particular sense of life and personal style. Pluto and Mickey Mouse were both humanized animals, with human-type brains. But Pluto's brain and style were more doglike than human. Mickey was a normal human boy in every way except his mouse ears and a disappearing tail. Pluto was always a dog. Once the animators understood this, they were good to go. If Mickey Mouse had gotten himself stuck on the flypaper the way that Pluto did, he would have handled the predicament altogether differently.

Body Language

I asked several animators what they would like to see in a book on the subject of Acting for Animators. How could I be most helpful? All but one suggested prominently that I include an encyclopedia of physiological movement—descriptions of movement that makes a character appear happy, anxious, sad, and angry. I've taken those suggestions and included a miniguide to generalized movement, but I do it with some reservations because good performance animation cannot be codified that way. Acting is not like a Chinese menu, where you take this facial expression from column A and that leg movement from column B. There are as many different body movements and facial expressions as there are characters. Each character is unique and has his own identity.

Suppose the character you are animating has a cold and you have to make her sneeze. How would you specify the action involved in a sneeze? Look under S in a book of facial expressions? You'd discover a garden-variety "Achoo!" But I know a woman who, when she sneezes, holds her nose and squeaks, evidently running the risk that she'll blow out her eardrums. By contrast, when I sneeze, it's so loud my wife says that I scare the dog. My point is that there is not a generic sneeze, nor a generic nose blow, any more than there is a generic way to scratch a mosquito bite. While it is true that these sorts of details will help bring a character to life, it is also true that nuance—and real illusion of life—resides in the *way* the details are drawn. And the *way* details are drawn have everything to do with the artist's perceptions of and attitudes about the world around him, coupled with his understanding of his character's value structure, physical attributes, and situational context.

Well-trained actors spend at least some of their time in dance studios. Having been an actor myself for thirty years, I have studied dance, mime, and Laban Movement Theory (discussed later in this chapter). But, as an actor, I can tell you that we do not think about movement the way animators do. Did you ever hear of a book entitled *The Inner Game of Tennis* (1974) by W. Timothy Gallwey? It's good stuff, and I recommend it. The main theme is that, if you want to play championship tennis, you need to stop thinking about your movement, your serve, and start thinking about where you want the ball to be. Yes, by all means, train well. But then, to move on to the next step, trust the training and focus on your goals and intention. That's the way actors consider movement. It's something you need to be able to do well, but it's not something you think about a lot. You see?

The mechanics of movement, important as it may be to animators, are second nature to actors. Actors learn to *allow* physical expression, not to *cause* it. It is actually an internal thing, not external. Internal impulses (thinking) are expressed externally, always through the body, sometimes through words. Try acting in a scene in which you move nothing but your face and see how far you get. Movement precedes words, but it is also true that, from an actor's perspective, if you are thinking about how you are moving, you will not be pursuing your objectives in the scene; you won't fully be playing your action. It's like when you ride a bike, you don't think about your feet pushing the pedals.

I have come to the conclusion that many animators have a misconception about how actors deal with movement. Preston Blair, for example, contends in *How to Animate Film Cartoons* that "the actor learns the craft—how to always walk or move with a meaning—to never pause unless you have a reason for it—when you pause, pause as long as you can. Hold a gesture as long as possible to let it register and sink-in" (1990, 14). With due respect to Mr. Blair, I know of nothing in the actor's lexicon about pausing for as long as you can. There is a rule of acting that says you ought not to move without a reason, without motivation, but that's it. The purpose of movement is destination. There's nothing in there about pausing as long as you can, but I understand that pauses take on physical properties for the animator. As my animator friend Doug Aberle observes, "Watch sometimes how long Daffy Duck may stare at the camera after being shot, before his face falls off." BIG pause! In general, however, sometimes you pause, and sometimes you don't. Depends on the moment and your objectives, and, most often, an actor is as surprised as everybody else when he pauses on stage.

Hayao Miyazaki, the Japanese animation master, talks about *ma*, the space that falls between the sound of claps when you clap your hands. He points out that *ma* is not an absence of something. It is very much something. He contends that American animators tend to be afraid of *ma*. They're afraid if they don't constantly have the sound of clapping going on, the audience will get bored. But Miyazaki pays close attention to *ma*. He fills it with emotion. He correctly observes that the audience will not leave you if the time is full. It does not have to always be full of sound. When Wile E. Coyote runs off a cliff and is suspended in thin air, he just hangs there for a long time before falling. That is *ma*, and it is wonderful. We empathize with his emotion.

Walt Disney discovered back in the 1930s that character expression is best when it involves the whole body, not just the face. Movement begins in the area of your navel and radiates outward into your limbs. Ask ten people what the most expressive part of their body is, and nine of them will tell you it's the face. The truth is that our hands and arms are the most expressive parts of our bodies. When you think of your body as a form, a block that is filling space, you see that only the head and face occupy a tiny part of the form. This lesson is hard for many new actors to grasp, coming as they do from the world of cinema where they are raised on the extreme facial close-up. "It's all in the eyes" is the maxim you hear all the time when you first learn about movie acting. It all comes to close-ups, and close-ups are about eyes. But that's no place to hang your hat if you are trying to understand human psychology and expression. This is why animators who rely too heavily on that mirror on the desk to work out facial expressions are doing only half the work. It is true that actors and animators must be masters of portraying emotion, but you do yourself a disservice if you believe that emotion is mainly expressed by the face. There was a famous review of Geraldine Page's Broadway performance in a Tennessee Williams play (*Summer and Smoke*, I think), in which the reviewer observed that "Miss Page does more acting with her back than most actors do with their fronts." So did Charlie Chaplin. And so it is—or should be—with animation. Get the body first, and *then* worry about the face!

When I was seventeen years old, I saw my first performance of *The Dark of the Moon* at Arena Stage in Washington, DC. Renee Auberjonois played the witch boy who falls in love with Barbara Allen, the human girl. He makes a deal with the head witch who allows him to become human on a trial basis. Now, the way most productions of this play deal with the transition from witch to human is with wild costumes. When the witch boy is a witch, he may have twigs growing out of his back for instance. And when he becomes human, the twigs are removed. Well, Renee Auberjonois did something in that show that made a dramatic impression on me as an actor and testifies to the power of visuals in human movement. He chose to move close to the ground when he was a witch, slinking around like a weasel, on all fours. After he made the deal with the head witch, he played subsequent scenes in increasingly erect postures. I recall that, at one point, he was tilted from the waist at about a 45-degree angle. Then, when he made his first entrance as a full human being, he walked out onto the stage standing fully erect, proud and tall. I get chills just thinking about it even now, almost forty years later! It was as if the lights in the theatre had gotten brighter. The actor had mimicked the evolution of man, from muck to full power. The words of the play were the same as I have now learned they are in every production. It was what that marvelous actor did with the physical movement that made the impression.

A person's physical movement is a compensation for, or reaction to, whatever is going on with him physically or psychically. Here's an example: I had an acting student in my San Francisco class who suffered from slipped discs in her spine. Invariably, she arrived at class late, walking slowly, and when she entered, she brought with her a pillow to sit on. Another student was a dancer, and I don't recall him ever sitting on a chair or sofa in the regular way. He preferred to sit cross-legged on the floor, back erect. Or, if he sat on a sofa, he would manage to position himself in a stretching pose. Mind you, none of this was done for effect. It's just the way he handled his body. Renee Auberjonois, in that play, decided that the power of the human was in the spine and in our evolutionary struggle to defy gravity.

With this proviso—that there really is not an ironclad, one-of-a-kind, check-off guide to physical movement—I offer the following generalities of body language for you to consider:

- Arms folded across the chest indicate that the person is "closed," intractable. Hands clasped behind one's back or folded across one's crotch indicate low-status, literally signaling that "I won't defend myself."

- Confidence manifests itself as relaxation, and relaxation manifests itself in a feeling of weight, not lightness. A confident character has weight, centeredness.

- A cerebral person will tend to lead with his forehead. A fun-loving person will tend to keep his chin up, exposing more throat. Children lead with their heads up a lot. Adults become more cerebral.

- A man with a beer gut has a lot of pressure on his lower back. When he sits in a chair, he will tend to use his arms and hands to ease the descent, perhaps bracing himself on the arms of the chair.

- When a person in conversation is interrupted, he may first turn his shoulders in the direction of the interruption before he turns his head, so he can complete whatever he is saying.

- Embarrassment is a low-status emotion, a way of defusing a tense moment. When you are embarrassed, you tend to shrink in space. You cast your gaze downward, your hands tend to rise to at least partly cover your face. Usually, when a person is embarrassed, he is acknowledging a truth of some kind. A kid tosses a ball through the living room window, and he's embarrassed. He did a bad thing. You discover that your fly is unzipped in front of the church group, and you are embarrassed. The top of your bathing suit comes off when you dive in the pool, and the resulting applause from onlookers embarrasses you.

- Anxiety is a heady energy, concentrated above the chest line and into the head. Woody Allen, to cite a popular example, typically displays a high power center, with arms and hands gesticulating wildly. This is a result of his philosophy of life. Woody operates on the premise that death is probably going to come sooner rather than later, and it makes him nervous. Mahatma Gandhi, on the other hand, presumably also knew that we all die, but he was comfortable with the idea, and so displayed a lower power center and gracefulness of movement.

- When body movements extend above the waist, above the shoulders, they are "light" in nature; body movements below the waist are more associated with "weight" or "heaviness." Gravity is pulling harder.

- As a person gets older, his spine settles, and the character begins to move in reaction to discomfort. When you see old people walking down the street with little mincing steps, it is because it would hurt them to take bigger steps. And note how very old people tend to keep their mouths open as they walk, perhaps to allow in more oxygen. When an elderly person turns to looks slightly behind him, he will turn his entire upper body, not just his neck. That's because of stiffness in the upper spine. I still remember my granddaddy, trying to back out of the driveway at his house in Atlanta. He shouldn't have been driving at all at his age, but they didn't use to make as big a deal about this as they do today. In order to drive in reverse, he didn't even attempt to turn his body around to look directly out the back window. That hurt his neck too much. So he watched the reverse-image in the rearview mirror as he accelerated carefully backward. That's not how they want you do to it at the DMV.

As I wrote the last sentence, a man in his thirties walked slowly by on the sidewalk outside my window. He wore one of those black elastic-and-Velcro girdlelike braces that you get at the chiropractor's office. He was angled forward from the waist, shifting his power center out in front of him until it tilted him forward and he had to catch up with himself. His arms did not have as much swing to them as they would typically. His neck was jutting out a bit, and his chin was angled up, parallel with the sidewalk. All in all, the movement seemed very uncomfortable, and it was all because of his reaction to whatever was going on with his back.

Power Centers

The notion of shifting power centers is a particularly useful tool for animators. The basic idea is that, when we stand and walk with ease, our power center is in our chest, leading us forward. Try it. Just get up and walk around the room in a relaxed fashion or, as I prefer to say, "with ease." Can you feel the power generating from your chest? Now, let the power center move into your stomach, dropping from your chest. A pregnant woman walks this way. Try moving the power center to your feet. Let it pull you along, shuffling. Suddenly, you feel like a street bum, a wino. Put the power center behind your neck and let it push you instead of pull you. Feel the energy acceler-

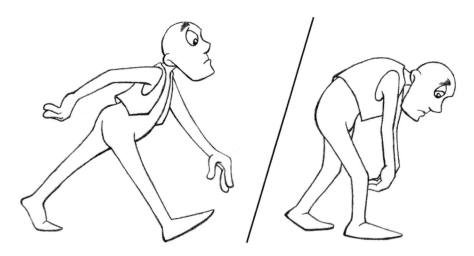

Every character has a power center

ate? Put the power center six inches over your head and dangle from it, let it make you dance.

In 1996, Michael Keaton starred in an underrated movie entitled *Multiplicity*, in which he played a man who clones himself in order to make life easier. "Two of me is better than one of me" is the logic. The thing is that the clones, all played by Keaton, have very different personalities. One is a macho kind of guy, another is politically correct and accommodating, and another is ultraweird and unpredictable, even zany. I recommend that you rent this movie and study what Keaton has accomplished, keeping in mind this business about power centers. The politically correct clone has a high power center, in his upper chest; the macho clone has a low power center, in his groin.

An anxious person has a power center in his head. Think of Woody Allen or the comedienne Joan Rivers. Did you ever see Woody Allen's movie, *Play It Again, Sam?* In it, Humphrey Bogart—a la *Casablanca*—appears in the Allen character's fantasy, instructing him on how to be a "real man," how to "get a dame." Allen's a nervous wreck, a man with a very heady energy, a high power center; Bogart, a man's man, has a very low power center, is unflappable.

Next time you're at a loss with a character you're animating, try shifting the power center.

The Psychological Gesture

Gestures do not always have to be illustrations of the spoken word. A gesture can express an inner emotional state. This is a particular trap for animators because the animation so often comes after the dialogue is recorded. The temptation is to listen to the prerecorded words and then have the gestures illustrate them. This is actually closer to mime than gesturing, and it is not an accurate mirror of what we humans do. Yes, we do sometimes gesture to illustrate, but we just as often gesture in a way that contrasts with the spoken word. Our gestures, in other words, can expose the truth within. I am convinced that the next generation of animation excellence will hinge on paying attention to just this kind of nuanced behavior.

Michael Chekhov is the person that first coined the acting term *psychological gesture*. (See *On the Technique of Acting* 1991). He contended that every character has a defining psychological

A psychological gesture can be a powerful acting tool

gesture. Have you ever noticed someone who wrings his hands a lot while he's talking? That's a psychological gesture. A bully punches someone in the chest with his finger. That's a psychological gesture. It is a useful concept for an animator.

For example, the word *broken* in the sentence "My heart is broken" can be expressed by miming the breaking of a stick. Try this experiment: With your hands down by your side, say that line out loud. Did you do it? Well, go ahead and do it. This lesson won't mean much unless you do the work. Say, right out loud, "My heart is broken." Nobody's watching. Good. Now, make the gesture of breaking that stick of wood. Good. Now say the line again and do the gesture at the same time, breaking the wood precisely when you say the word *broken*. See how much stronger the line sounds, how much stronger it feels? Now, put your hands in your pocket or down by your side, say the line out loud and *imagine* breaking that stick. Make the stick-breaking gesture mentally. The line still sounds stronger, just as if you were actually, physically making the gesture with your hands out front. Amazing, huh?

Now let's take the notion of the psychological gesture a step further, incorporating Chekhov's concept of "atmosphere." Imagine a car wreck on a highway. Police cars are in attendance, lights flashing in the drizzly early evening air. There is a yellow tarp covering what must be a body in one of the wrecked cars. A man is sitting on the curb, sobbing. Got the picture? Okay, now imagine that you arrive on the scene, on foot. Can you feel the "atmosphere" of the place? It's quite different from the atmosphere in the coffee shop down the street or the atmosphere at a playground. Notice how your body reacts to the very idea of atmosphere at that car wreck scene? Notice how you tense up? There is a valuable acting lesson there. There is an inherent atmosphere in every scene, every setting. Rather than simply entering a scene as if you (or your character) are all that exists in the world, let the atmosphere of the scene inform you emotionally. React to it, factor it into your actions. Let it color the intentions you bring into the scene. This principle is what makes haunted house scenarios so scary, by the way. The atmosphere is designed to scare the pants off you.

Take a look at some drawings by Daumier, a man who obviously understood the principle, too. For every mood there is a gesture.

Effect of Alcohol and Drugs on Movement

Alcohol and marijuana relax the muscles, causing the character to yield to the pull of gravity. A drunk character is heavy, and his movement is slower, the arcs more fluid. Cocaine will wire the character, causing him to doubly resist the pull of gravity, and his movement will be swifter, the arcs quicker.

Acting-wise, you can lump all external substances, whether they stimulate or depress, together under this maxim: Allow the substance to do whatever that particular substance does to the body—and then act to control it, to hide it. If it relaxes you and slows you down, strive for alertness and muscle tension; if it wires you, like cocaine, strive to relax, to moderate your behavior.

A drunken person—unless he is *trying* to be drunk, like at a frat party or with a bunch of drunken sailors—will act against the loss of control. The person who drinks too much at office parties, or on a date, circumstances where it is a liability to appear too out-of-control, are worth studying. Even as a person is getting mentally and physically slower, he strives to appear alert, even erudite. It is a hallmark of the amateur actor that, when he plays a drunk, he stumbles and mumbles across the stage, really layering it on. For an accurate, dramatic live-action depiction of drunken behavior, watch the Jack Lemmon movie *The Days of Wine and Roses*. For a comedic live-action depiction, watch Dudley Moore's performance in *Arthur*.

Pantomime

Pantomime is one of those words that can lead to confusion because there is "English Pantomime," which involves fairy tales and cross-dressing, and there is the kind of pantomime for which Marcel Marceau is famous. The origins of both are unclear, but they evidently are rooted in Commedia dell 'Arte in sixteenth century Italy. The Harlequin character got into the act somewhere along the way, donning whiteface, to emphasize facial expression. Today, an informal man-on-the-street poll will surely show that most civilians consider pantomime to be a kind of wordless acting—something very distinct from the acting you see in movies. Consider this: An actor expresses

A mime generally does not speak at all

love with words, sighs, and accompanying gestures. A mime generally does not speak at all, so he expresses love with poses, attitudes—maybe he will cross his hands across his heart and put a funny expression on his face.

The way the word *pantomime* is used in the world of animation is probably a holdover from the days of the silent cartoons. Back then, the characters *did* use pantomime! But that's because they had no voices, no other way to communicate. All that changed when talkies came in! Today, it is common for the animator—particularly in feature animation—to listen to a prerecorded voice track, making his animation fit the voices. And when you do that, you're really not pantomiming. You're looking for the motivation underneath the words. Remember that words express thoughts. If the animator is trying to pantomime the words he is hearing, he is going to wind up trying to physically convey the words in a wordless way. Words, movement, and emotion do not fit together like that, even in animation.

Stage actors don't pantomime and, in fact, it is considered to be bad acting if they do. It is too external, too much of an "indication" of emotion rather than a straightforward expression of it. The movement in pantomime is very—for lack of a better word—artful, and the audience relates to it differently than they do to the general movement of actors. There is an added mental step in pantomime. Part of the appreciation is in the "considered" nature of the movement.

Charlie Chaplin considered himself to be a pantomime, which he defined as a performer who would use mute gestures and facial expressions to convey emotion. That's because he worked in silent pictures but, frankly, I think he underestimated himself. He was far more than a mime. Chaplin always was a powerful actor, attuned to generating a sense of empathy in his international audience. Taking his self-assessment at face value, however, may explain why his stardom diminished with the advent of sound in motion pictures. To be sure, sound is what killed certain animated, pantomimed characters, like Felix the Cat. And other silent stars like Harry Langdon and Buster Keaton did not make the transition because they mainly practiced pantomime. In Chaplin's autobiography, he bemoans the arrival of sound pictures, and he delayed his participation in it for as long as he could.

As we have already discussed, acting has very little to do with words anyway. It's all about intention, motivation, actions—emotion. But if character movement takes the form of pantomime, you've crossed over into another distinct art form.

Laban Movement Theory

Rudolf Laban (1879–1958) was a major pioneer in the Central European Expressionist Art modern dance movement. He developed a new and influential approach to the study of dance, focusing on the systematic analysis of movement in relation to the dynamic use of the body in space. He also created a widely used form of notation (now evolved into Labanotation) to describe movement. Laban's work was revolutionary in its day and has subsequently been applied to a wide variety of disciplines, from psychotherapy to ethnology, from movement therapy to voice training, acting, and dance and, during the past several years, to computer animation. Although there is no school or teacher offering specific Laban movement training for animators at this time, animator and Certified Laban Movement Analyst Leslie Bishko, Director of the Computer Animation Program at Vancouver Institute of Media Arts in Canada, has written several papers on the application of Laban Movement Analysis (LMA) to computer animation methods. She includes analogies between Laban's Effort theory and the twelve Animation Principles. I am indebted to Ms. Bishko and to Jean Newlove of the Jean Newlove Centre for Laban Studies in London for their assistance in preparing the following primer.

Before getting into Laban theory itself, a brief historical preface is helpful because Rudolf Laban's original ideas have been interpreted, reinterpreted, and synthesized in different ways in different parts of the world at different times by different folks. Jean Newlove studied personally with Rudolf Laban in the 1940s, worked as his assistant and is familiar with what the man himself had to say. She is the author of an excellent book on the subject, entitled *Laban for Actors and Dancers* (1993). Her school offers a diploma course in which students study Laban in depth, using it as a base for most theatre skills. Simultaneous with Newlove's career in the UK and Europe, however, Laban's theories found their way to the United States through other disciples. Imgard Bartenieff in particular mixed her perspectives with Laban's and created Laban Movement Analysis (LMA), a theoretical framework for movement observation and description for which one can receive certification through the Laban/Bartenieff Institute of Movement Studies in New York. Graduates from this school have fanned out across the United States and Canada and have, in turn, trained others. Animator Leslie Bishko studied the LMA branch of Laban, not Laban theory as espoused by Ms. Newlove. While there are differences in terminology and focus between the North American and British versions of Laban theory, their roots are very similar.

That's enough history. Let's roll up our sleeves and get to work. I can't possibly do justice to this very rich resource in these few pages, but I want to give you the basic ideas behind Laban theory, plus a list of resources for further study.

It is difficult to talk about movement because it is constantly changing. Imagine the challenge you would face if you had to write a paper describing in detail how a child's body is moving as he pedals his tricycle up and down the driveway. He's pedaling like crazy, then he slows down, and then he topples over as he tries to make a U-turn. At every point, the nature of his movement changes. The genius of Rudolf Laban is that he defined a set of movement categories, with parameters within each category. These parameters provide a frame of reference for the observation and description of movement. In this chapter, I introduce two categories: *space* (i.e., where the movement is happening), and *effort* (i.e., how intention and will affect movement).

The CD-ROM that accompanies this book contains a picture of a twenty-sided object called an *icosahedron*. Along with the tetrahedron and three others, the icosahedron is one of Plato's solids, and it is at the base of Rudolf Laban's theories.

Space

Imagine that you have created an animated character that looks like a regular-sized brick with arms and legs, and it is standing in the icosahedron. In Laban terminology, the personal space around your character is called its *kinesphere*—the distance it can extend its arms and its free leg if it is balancing on one leg. Your character can move to any of the points of the icosahedron. Actually, your character can move in infinite ways but, for the purposes of this chapter—and for simplicity's sake—I will reduce this to the most basic six movements: (1) forward, (2) backward, (3) up, (4) down, (5) sideways/left, (6) sideways/right. Forward/backward movement occurs on the sagittal axis; up/down movement occurs on the vertical axis; left/right movement occurs on the horizontal axis. As Leslie Bishko observes, "the axis are directly analogous to the Cartesian coordinate system's X, Y, and Z axis, used in computer animation."

Effort

Effort refers to *how* the character moves through space. He can move in different ways, depending on how you vary his inner attitude toward space, time, and weight. Each character you create is unique and moves in his or her own way, right? He can move on a Time scale measured from very fast urgency to very lingering slowness; he mobilizes his Weight with forceful strength or delicate lightness, and his attention toward Space can be direct, like an arrow, or indirect, like a mangled figure-eight. Plus there is the variable of Flow, a factor that pertains to the "feeling" of movement and can be measured on a scale that ranges from Bound to Free. When a baseball pitcher winds up for a pitch, for example, his movement has a Bound quality. It has resistance, a pause, and then the ball is hurled across home plate with Free Flow, as if he is trying to throw the ball straight through the catcher's mitt.

Let's look a little closer at the Time factor, break it down a little further. This offers a way to differentiate between the *qualities* of time (sudden, urgent or sustained, lingering), and *quantitative* time (fast, slow, accelerating, decelerating). If the brick character you created walks down a city street, his movement may be sudden (urgent) or sustained (lingering), accelerating or decelerating depending on circumstance. If he steps around a pothole, he may slow down; or he may speed up to make a traffic light. This being the case, both Leslie Bishko and Jean Newlove prefer to refer to the Time continuum as one ranging from suddenness to sustainment, with the presumption that the character may, while moving suddenly or sustained, vary between fast and slow.

It is useful to think of Effort as the character's "inner attitude" toward the movement factors of Space, Weight, Time, and Flow. It's not the mass of the thing or character that makes the difference, but the character's attitude toward how it moves. For example, when considering Weight, the character can have an Active or Passive attitude toward mobilization of his body weight. Imgard Bartenieff (LMA) is the one who originally came up with the distinctions between Active and Passive. As she put it, "Lightness in Passive Weight becomes Limp; Strong Passive Weight becomes Heaviness, giving in." The British version of Laban does not use these terms, preferring Rudolf's original *resisting* or *indulging*. But regardless of the precise terminology, you get the idea. The character can be active or passive, give in to or resist movement.

Does your character move with quick, flicking motions or with slow, purposeful movement? There are eight possible combinations of Space, Time, Weight, and Flow, all of which are demonstrated by an actor who appears in the CD-ROM that accompanies this book. If we remove Flow from the equation, which has to do with the emotional or "feeling" aspects of movement, we wind up with the following basic types of movement:

Press   (direct, sustained, strong)

Wring   (indirect, sustained, strong)

Glide   (direct, sustained, light)

Float   (indirect, sustained, light)

Thrust   (direct, sudden, strong)

Slash   (indirect, sudden, strong)

Dab   (direct, sudden, light)

Flick   (indirect, sudden, light)

The best and easiest way to really grasp how this works is to get up on your feet and move around the room. Reading about Laban is like reading about bicycle riding. It's all well and good to know how the chain goes 'round and 'round, but, at some point, you need to get up on the bike to really grasp what it means to ride the thing. I know it looks silly to dance around the room, but forget about that. You're an artist, and artists are already thought to be a bit odd. Anyway, if somebody walked in and found an animator doing her facial expression thing in front of a mirror, all bets would be off.

First, just relax and walk with ease from one side of the room to the other, like your regular self. Don't try to be a character or to otherwise change yourself. Be aware of your body as you move through the space.

Now let's transfer your weight and keep walking. When we talk about varying the "weight" of a character, we're referring to a tension that exists between gravity and upward movement. Relaxation equates to weight. Totally relax, and you'll fall down on the ground. A drunken person is relaxed, pulled down by gravity. When you are having an energetic day, your energy will lift you up, pushing away from gravity. Exuberance pushes you away from gravity.

Press (direct, sustained, and strong)

Let's work on Pressing. Think of it like pushing a friend's stalled car off to the side of the road. Direct, sustained, strong. See? Do it. You'd push a car differently than you would a shopping cart, which would be closer to Gliding.

Now try Wringing. Suppose you are a soaking towel. If you wring yourself out, you do so in an indirect, sustained, and strong manner.

Floating is what it sounds like it is. Balloons float. Remember boxer Muhammed Ali in his prime? "I float like a butterfly, sting like a bee!" he used to shout in the ring. In Laban terms, Muhammed would be Floating (indirect + sustained + light), and then thrusting (direct + sudden + strong), maybe interspersed with Flicking (indirect + sudden + light).

If you were a cotton ball being dabbed onto somebody's face, how would you move? What is Dabbing? Direct, sudden, and light. Got it?

From the animator's perspective, movement is the visible outer result of the character's inner impulses. If you animate that brick character you created earlier, causing him to walk in a jaunty, brisk, and determined fashion, light on his feet, chest out, the person viewing the animation would presume this is a happy character. This movement could be described as Dabbing. Are you starting to see how Laban can be used?

Phrasing, which is a term much used by Leslie Bishko, refers to the rhythmic changes of movement in an animated character. Changes of Effort over time can be phrased in the following ways:

Even	continuous, unchanging
Increasing	from lesser to greater intensity, accelerating
Decreasing	from greater to lesser intensity, decelerating
Accented	series of accents
Vibratory	series of sudden, repetitive movements
Resilient	series of rebounding, resilient movements (Maletic 1984)

Applying this quality to the animated brick walking down the street, we could say his phrasing is *even*, perhaps *increasing* if you want to show a growing sense of urgency.

In a conversation I had with Leslie Bishko when preparing this chapter, she said, "My teaching is infused with LMA-esque scrutiny of animated movement. The LMA themes that come up over and over again are Initiation/Sequencing and Phrasing. In particular, the phrase Anticipation-Squash/Stretch-Follow-through-Overlapping is a practical example of LMA's phrasing principle of Preparation/Action/Recuperation. I also discuss the elasticity of Squash and Stretch in relationship to Breath and Shape changes in the torso to help students understand how they can phrase their use of Squash and Stretch to convey emotion" (Bishko 1999).

Laban theory is a big, important, and largely unexplored subject for both animators and actors. It is my fervent hope that the publication of this book will spur more research and further application. Jean Newlove's orientation is with motivation for actors and dancers, artists who get up on their feet and actually move through space. The actor in me responds powerfully to this perspective. Leslie Bishko's LMA orientation is with computer animators, artists who manipulate characters on a screen. Her goal is to create an industry-standard computer animation interface based on LMA—a way for animators to better describe and analyze movement. The work of both, however, is about how the mind/body expressive processes manifest themselves in movement and, with both acting and animation, that is Ground Zero.

Speech
6

Acting has very little to do with words. Words express a thought, the same as a hug or a kiss. What we are really searching for in acting is intention, objectives, motivation, and emotion. In other words, acting is more about what is *underneath* the words. Remember the metaphor of the iceberg: Only 15 percent of it shows above the water line; 85 percent is under the water. But in order for it to be an iceberg, you still have to have the unseen 85 percent.

Animators who work in feature films have a tough job because the character voices are typically recorded before the animation is created. In the real world, movement precedes words. When a thought occurs, it is not the words that emerge first, it is head and eye movement, shoulder and neck movement. Therefore, when animating to pre-recorded dialogue, the animator is forced to sort of work backward from the way actual actors work, finding the inner impulse—the thought—that would be expressed by the recorded words. In the instant before a character speaks, he moves, expressing the impulse. Watch the way ventriloquists make their dummies move around, looking this way and that, generally a beat ahead of the mouth movement.

Here's a trick I use all the time in my regular acting classes, one that may help you find the key to animating a prerecorded voice. Listen for the most awkward or most difficult or most unusual word or phrase in a scene. Isolate it and say it out loud yourself. Try to find in yourself the impulse, which would allow you to express this way. If you can justify that, you can probably hang the rest of the character on it. Let's say you're listening to a voice track in which a male character says, at one point, "Oh, goody, goody, goody!" Now, you probably don't walk around in your daily life saying that. It wouldn't be cool. But try it on for size. Get up from your chair and walk around the room, saying out loud, "Oh, goody, goody, goody!" You'll discover that the impulse comes from a high place in the body, for starters, and you'll probably want to purse your lips when you say it. The character is a lip purser who carries his energy up in the shoulder and neck area. Also, keep in mind when you are animating a prerecorded dialogue track that movement and emotion are a two-way street. Emotion makes you move a certain way, and the way you move will make you feel a certain way.

Since the audience expects to hear dialogue once the impulse to speak is evident, there is comedy to be found in putting a delay between the impulse and the actual audible sound. Find the impulse to speak, but then don't speak. Hold the impulse, ride it like a pony. The audience will hang on the moment with great expectancy. If you have a prerecorded track, it's difficult to use this one because the timing is already built in, but maybe one day you'll get the chance. I recall years ago seeing a production of William Sayoran's *The Time of your Life*. One of the characters had a philosophical and rather nonsensical short speech to give: "What? What not? No foundation, all the way down the line," he was supposed to say. The actor playing the role stretched that one sequence into maybe a minute and a half of hysterically funny shifting inner impulses. He would find the impulse to say something, go slightly into the predictor-movement, then decide not to say that, changing the impulse to another thought and predictor-movement, then deciding not to say that. And of course, by the time he finally finished, what he said hadn't made much sense anyway. It was fall-down-on-the-floor funny. Try it yourself. You can hold an audience on the tip of your fingers for a very long time this way. If they feel you are about to say something, they'll hang in there with you. I've never seen an animator use the lesson, but there is no reason why it would not work there, too.

Active Listening

Imagine a scene set in Washington Square Park in New York, on a sunny summer morning. The characters are two middle-aged women who are sitting next to one another on a bench, talking about their kids who are playing in the fountain. They take turns talking, sometimes interrupting one another. The trick to making this kind of transaction come alive is active listening. When Woman #1 talks, Woman #2 does more than just sit there, absorbing. Woman #2 is listening, projecting ahead, filling in blanks that are left unsaid, framing responses, deciding not to interrupt, and keeping an eye on her kid. In other words, listening, when it is right, is extremely active.

Active listening

Actor Nicol Williamson tells a story about when he was a young actor, playing his first large role. In the play, his character first entered a party scene at the top of the play, but he didn't speak any lines for two pages. After a run-through, the director was giving notes to the assembled cast. "Nicol, what are you doing during your first entrance, after you enter the party?" "You mean before I speak? I'm not doing anything really, just listening." "Wrong," said the director. "You're listening, coming up with responses to what is being said—and then deciding not to say them." The point is that, even for those two pages of non-speaking, it was essential for the actor to be *doing* something. If a tornado had blown through the evil Queen's palace while she was stirring her bubbling, festering pot of poison, she would have had to stop doing what she was doing and deal with the storm, close windows and such. She would then be playing another action, this one not in pursuit of being the fairest one of all, but of staying alive. Once secure, she would return to her poisons and her evil objectives.

When one character listens to another, he should still be doing something. In fact, your character should be doing something 100 percent of the time when he is on stage. *Doing* means playing an action, pursuing an objective. Scratching an ear or crossing a leg is also doing something, but that's not what I mean. To *do* something, theatrically speaking, is to play an action, to have intention, to pursue an objective.

The Camera

7

Acting for Camera

In live-action movies, the reaction shot carries 90 percent of the baggage. It is so important, in fact, that many live-action actors view the master shot as little more than a rehearsal for the close-ups. When editing a movie, the editor usually cuts to reaction shots. In close-up coverage of a shot, in fact, they learn to "listen, react, speak"—being careful not to overlap lines. This is so the editors can get a clean edit on the sound track and will have reaction shots to cut to.

The basic set up for a filmed live-action scene is a "master shot," which includes the action of the entire scene, plus "coverage"—close-ups this way and close-ups that way. It is all put together in the editing room. An animated movie, of course, doesn't shoot the same way. It's not necessary to make an animated master shot for an entire scene, plus entire-scene close-ups. You lay all that out on the story board in the first place, essentially editing beforehand. But, to the extent that an animated feature film follows live-action film editing technique, it is useful to talk for a minute about the way actors in live-action approach the process. The performance they give in a master shot is different from what they do in a close-up.

A master shot is usually photographed from some distance, anywhere from a few feet to the length of a football field. The further away the shot is, the more physical the actor can—and must—be. It is okay to gesture a lot, for example, if the master shot is staged across the distance of a department store parking lot. At that distance, the actor would think of it as delivering a performance that is almost as large as what he might do on the Broadway stage.

The closer the camera gets to the actor, the more still the performance needs to be. In an extreme close-up, when you have a full screen of the actor's face, everything is in the eyes, so you don't want to have the character's head shaking around too much. The camera sees thoughts. The audience and other characters will likely look first at the eyes for clues about emotional state. One caveat: In your effort to make the character hold still, be careful that you don't lower the emotional stakes! This is a common error made by new actors when they first start acting for camera. The intention is the same as in the long shot, the stakes remain high, but the *focus* of the performance is different.

The point is this: When you are animating a sequence that includes long shots and close-ups, remember that the actor behaves differently depending on the shot. You don't simply take the action from the long shot and blow it up because, if you do, the physical action would be too frenetic in close-up. Make the performance the right size for the frame of the shot.

Elia Kazan, the director of such classic movies as *A Streetcar Named Desire, On the Waterfront,* and *East of Eden,* says that the camera doesn't just look at the actor, it looks inside him (1988, 256). What he means by this is that the camera sees the tapestry of thoughts and emotions inside the character. One of my favorite contemporary movie actors is Kevin Spacey (*The Usual Suspects, American Beauty*). The thing that makes him so good on camera is the way he performs in close-up. When the camera cuts to him for a reaction, it typically sees the reaction, and then his reaction evolves into yet another thought. It's mental and emotional movement, caught on film. This mental fluidity makes him appear more interesting than the line of the script might suggest.

The Actor Generally Leads the Camera

The camera's perspective in a master shot is usually that of an audience. Camera movement led by the actor's gaze or shift of attention. For example, consider the following scene:

Master Shot: A woman sits alone at a table in a restaurant alone waiting for someone. She glances at her watch. Move in for medium-close shot so we pick up her facial expression. Whoever she is waiting for is late. Off camera, we hear a female voice: "Sorry I'm late. . . ." The woman at the table reacts to the voice and looks toward the door. Cut to: Woman's POV of friend approaching table. Or, the camera might pan toward the door, off the woman's glance, picking up her friend as she enters the scene.

Now suppose the scene had been shot this way: Same master shot. Same medium-close up. But instead of hearing the friend's greeting from off-camera while the on-screen shot captures the seated woman's reaction, we quick-cut to the woman at the door, entering. She sees her friend at the table and, off her recognition, she calls out, "Sorry I'm late. . . ." Then we cut to the woman at the table, reacting to the arrival of her friend.

We could do it either way and the scene would work, but we'd have to put in the reaction shots somewhere.

Imagine a scene in a haunted house, late afternoon. Our hero climbs the creaking wooden steps, pushes thick cobwebs aside, and steps into the main entrance hall. Silence and gloom. Slow pan around the room from our hero's POV, sunlight casting odd-shaped shadows through the dust. Cut back to the hero, taking in the room, smelling the mustiness. Suddenly, a large bat comes to life in the rafters, his flapping wings in turn disturbing some nesting birds that fly into action, squawking. Cut to our alarmed hero, reacting to the noise, looking around anxiously. Cut back to the room. Birds fly out a broken window, the bat settles back into the rafters. Cut back to the hero. His face, now touched with a glaze of perspiration, relaxes. He chuckles at his own skittishness and continues cautiously into the house.

Technique 8

Technique is a potpourri category of acting dos and don'ts. An actor learns, for example, that if a scene is going south, if he's starting to hear people in the audience coughing and shuffling around, the worst thing to do is to "chase" them, that is, to increase the intensity of the performance. It will only make things worse. It is preferable to stop, reconnect with your intention, and scene partner—and the audience will return. In shorthand: "Don't chase your audience!" Animators, of course, don't have this sort of problem to solve because animation isn't presented to an audience in real-time, but there are many snippets of acting wisdom that I think you will be able to use in animation.

If you read entertainment industry trade publications, you'll see advertisements for acting teachers who teach Meisner Technique or Adler Technique or even Stanislavsky Technique. Lee Strasberg's Method Acting could be called a technique. None of this means much except that each teacher advocates his own approach to acting and has slapped his name on it in order to sell more seats in their classes. There is in reality no single, correct technique. Technique is whatever works.

Simplify Your Actions

The more direct, simple, and specific your acting choices are, the better. Trying to play, for example, "I want to be loved," is neither active nor specific enough. A stronger choice would be "I want you to go on a date with me" or "I want you to marry me." It might be true that your character desires love and affection, which gives voltage to the way he tries to get a date, but it is a weak acting choice to play the general need instead of the specific action.

Avoid Ambivalence

When you have to animate a character that is having an indecisive moment, it is stronger to have him shift between two strong convictions than it is for him to be ambivalent. In other words, if your character is uncertain whether to kiss the girl, it is best to have him commit 100 percent to "Yes! I'm going to do it!"—and then have him take a 180 in the other direction with "No! What am I doing? Am I crazy?!" The alternative is to have him just sit there, his internal dialogue being, "Oh me, oh my! I don't know what to do." Shifting back and forth between strong decisions, even if it is done lightning-quick, is more dynamic acting-wise. Imagine a character that comes to a fork in the road. Which way to go? Left or right? Mentally, switch back and forth until a decision is made, just like switching a light switch on and off and on again.

Make strong choices

Never Deny the Reality of Your Scene Partner

This is a stage actor note that I think might have some relevance to animation. It is spin on two other acting notes: "Acting is doing; acting is reacting" and "Stay in the present moment." Now, animators of course do not have a present moment. In animation, there is only the indication of a present moment. However, your character has what appears to the audience to be a present moment. If Minny is cozying up to Mickey, she is presumably being sensitive to how Mickey is reacting to her advances. If he reacts with eagerness, she will act one way; if he resists her, she will react another way. If this scene were being played by live actors, the notion of staying in the present moment and playing off the reality of what your scene partner is doing would be very clear. But we're doing animation. I almost didn't include this particular note, but I'm gambling that my readers will grasp what I am getting at. You can't have one character carry forward with an action while being oblivious to the reaction of the other character in the scene. Well, you can, if that's part of the joke. But as an acting rule, the characters need to play off one another. They need to be reactive and to deal with the reality of whatever their scene partner is doing.

What Kind of Animal Would Your Character Be?

This acting note is kin to finding power centers in your character. Instead of thinking power center, think of your human character as an animal. What kind of animal would he be? Marlon Brando in *A Streetcar Named Desire* is using the image of an ape in order to find the rhythm and grace of his character, Stanley Kowalski. When I saw Tommy Lee Jones portray the lawman in the movie *The Fugitive*, I noticed that whenever he was close to Harrison Ford the fugitive, he would raise his head and sniff the air, just like a wolf. This animal-like behavior worked well for his character. Alma in Tennessee Williams' play *Summer and Smoke* is high strung, skittish, and birdlike, maybe like a stork or heron, wary but regal. Dustin Hoffman had an early triumph in the movie *Midnight Cowboy*. His character, Ratso Rizzo, actually moves like a rat. He tilts forward in his walk, leading

What animal would your character be?

with his nose and his small beady eyes. That's not an accident. Hoffman frequently uses animal images in his characterizations. Now that I've mentioned it to you, keep an eye out for that when you watch his movies.

For the animator, this principle can be used two ways. If the character you are animating is an animal, ask yourself what kind of *human* would he be. An owl that behaves like Joe Pesci did in *Goodfellas* would be very funny, I suspect.

Remember the Fruit Salad

After watching an actress perform in a scene at the Actor's Studio, Lee Strasberg determined that she was making an acting error, playing the end of the scene at the beginning. In other words, she was ahead of herself, anticipating what was coming up. As she stood on stage, awaiting his sage advice, he asked her an odd question. "Do you know how to make a fruit salad?" She figured she hadn't heard him correctly. "Excuse me?" "A fruit salad," he repeated, "Do you know how to make one?" "Well, yes." "How do you do it?" The actress was nonplussed, aware that the entire packed room was watching her, asked if he wanted her to tell him precisely how to make a fruit salad. She could not fathom how this line of questioning had anything at all to do with her acting. "Yes," said Strasberg. "How do you do it?" "Umm . . . well, I peel a banana. . . ." She paused. "Yes? A banana? Then what?" "Well, I cut up some strawberries and a few grapes, maybe put in some grapefruit, perhaps a peach. . . ." "And then you have a fruit salad, right?" asked Strasberg, peering at the girl through his thick glasses. "Uh-huh." "And you can't have a fruit salad until you do all of those things, right?" "Right." "Until you have done all those things, you don't have a fruit salad?" "Right." "Good," Strasberg beamed. "That's the mistake you were making with that scene. You were trying to have a fruit salad before you had done all the things with the fruit."

When you are animating a character, it is absolutely essential that he go through all of the thoughts that the scene calls for. No shortcuts. You can have the thoughts come through lightning-quick, but they must all be there. This is a very important acting lesson. Remember Strasberg's fruit salad, and do not play the end of the scene before you get there. Suppose an actor is working on a character for a Jell-O commercial, and he has to take a bite and say, "Yum!" The thought process goes this way: As the spoon comes toward the mouth, the character is looking forward to the bite based on his preconceived idea of what Jell-O tastes like. There is expectation. Once he takes the Jell-O into his mouth, there is a moment of tasting, after which the communication goes to the brain. Jell-O is good! From the brain, the word *Yum!* comes out the mouth. You see what I mean? It's not a simple matter of "spoon in—big grin—spoon out—*Yum!*" There is a sequence of thoughts and reactions that come with the taste.

Live Action Reference

Feature animation usually involves animating the characters after the voice track is recorded. And most voice-over sessions are videotaped for later reference. The animator can watch the tape and observe the body language and facial expressions of the actor when he actually recorded the words. This is a valuable live-action reference, but it has some limitations that are worth mentioning.

Speaking now as an actor who had done my share of voice-over work, I'm here to tell you that what an actor does with a line in front of a microphone in a recording studio is not necessarily what he would do with that same line if he was playing a scene on location or on stage. A lot of the variable comes from the recording session necessity that the actor remain close to the microphone and not to make extraneous noises. The engineers want a clean track. What this means is that actors who are doing voice recordings will focus all of their bodily energy in support of the words being recorded—instead of playing off the reality of an actual scene partner. I, for example, will use my arms and hands far more in a recording session than I might in the actual playing of a scene with another actor. And my face will tend to be more animated because I'm trying to summon up 100 percent of the emotion that might be expressed by the words I'm recording. An actor in a recording session is, in a way, playing with himself, and the animator is wise to take this into consideration when watching videotapes of his performance.

Rotoscoping

Rotoscoping—making a direct copy or tracing of a filmed or taped live-action performance—is, by definition, a second-generation performance, so you're already swimming upstream if you want to create a sense of theatrical spontaneity in the animation. And, if that isn't troubling enough, there is the real possibility that the original live-action performance you are rotoscoping lacked a "feeling for acting" in the first place. Directing live actors is a special art in itself, hard enough to do when the final goal is to put the live-action performances up on the screen. But to direct live action with the goal of having it later copied into animation . . . wow! That's tough. If the director of a live-action sequence is oriented to the final animation—in other words, if he is focusing on the ultimate performance of the animators instead of focusing on the in-the-present-moment performance of the live actors—he may be tempted to push for lots of physical movement, even if it is not motivated acting-wise.

There is a real trap waiting in the capture of live-action movement for movement's sake, especially if it is segregated from theatrical intention and the actor-audience contract. It is sort of like studying the movement of a person riding a bicycle without taking into consideration where he is going on the bike. Legs move up and down, body hunkers over the handle bars, breath goes in and out of lungs. . . . But a person who is riding to town to fetch the doctor is going to ride that bike a whole lot differently from someone who is riding a stationary bike at a health club. Intention affects emotion, emotion affects movement.

Disney animators Frank Thomas and Ollie Johnston, in their book, *The Illusion of Life*, talk despairingly about their efforts with rotoscoping. "Whenever we stayed too close to the Photostats, or directly copied even a tiny piece of human action, the results looked very strange. The moves appeared real enough, but the figure lost the illusion of life." "The point is," they continue, "a work of art is never a copy; for it to have meaning to people of many generations and numerous cultures, it must be the personal statement of the artist" (Thomas and Johnston 1981, 252–53). Indeed. The illusion of life is in the character's emotion and the artist's interpretation of reality—not in the isolated movement of various body parts.

Mocap

Motion Capture, otherwise known in the trade as *mocap*, is a CG descendant of rotoscope, which was invented by Max Fleischer for 2-D purposes. It involves the wiring up of a live actor, dancer, or mime with sensors so that his movements are converted into a digitized computer map. He raises his left arm, and, on the screen, the image raises its left arm. He shakes his head, and the image shakes its head. Once the performance is thus captured, it falls to the animator to take the computer image and enhance it, to make it into animation. The basic movement is already taken care of, so the animator just has to fill in the blanks, so to speak. The public is supposed to be none the wiser, and the entire enterprise is said to be a big money-saver for the producers.

Most animators actively hate mocap because it puts them into a secondary position creatively. The live performers have already delivered the essence—and, what is worse, the live performance itself may well be lacking if its focus is on movement rather than performance. In some of the live action that was rotoscoped for Disney's feature film *Pocahontas*, for example, the actress was actually a dancer. When she walked across the room in some the live-action reference scenes, she did so like a dancer—toes out, ball-of-foot down first—not like a regular person.

Motion Capture is used widely in computer games and, in feature films, for background crowd scenes (*Titanic* is a good example) and stunts (*Batman*). It is controversial because so many grandiose, even incorrect claims have been made about its virtues as a cost-saving replacement for the character animator. The truth is that mocap can be very expensive and is not at all a replacement for the character animator. Also, it comes with a number of limitations, mainly that you can only use it for human figures. You can't capture a human and then turn that into animation for an animal. Further, you can't capture the motion of a skinny person and turn it into animation for a fat person because weight moves differently with skinny and fat.

For an excellent overview and history of motion capture, I strongly recommend *Understanding Motion Capture for Computer Animation and Video Games* (2000) by Alberto Menache. Alberto has been working with motion capture for many years, and his book is the most eloquent and final word on the subject.

There isn't much I can do except commiserate with animators who have to clean up and enhance a mocap performance, but I'd like to share a few thoughts with the folks who direct the live-action performances in the first place.

Actors perform for audiences. The thing that actors do *presumes* an audience. Acting is an interpretative art, from actor to audience. So when you are directing performers for mocap (or video reference), ask yourself these questions, even if you are working on a kick boxing computer game:

1. What does the character want? What does he/she need?

2. What is the character's relationship with the other performers?

3. What is the "moment before"? In other words, where did the character come from when he entered the scene?

4. What is the "moment after"? In other words, where is the character going after he leaves the scene?

5. Where is the audience in relation to the performer? Actors play for an audience, one way or the other, even if they are acting in movies. Even though you may want to capture a lot of motion on the computer, it will help to tell the performer where the audience is.

6. Where is the negotiation in the scene?

Character Rhythm

You can actually tap out a person's or character's inner rhythm with a pencil on the desk. A sloth or snail would have, naturally, a much slower inner rhythm than a woodpecker.

The point is that the rhythm of a character can change based on circumstances. What happens, do you figure, when a sloth gets angry? Same inner rhythm? I don't think so. The sloth won't suddenly start jumping around like a rabbit, and he probably will still move about a foot a day—but you should be able to tell by looking at him that his inner rhythm has increased. It would be in the eyes, maybe the set of the jaw.

The Look of Memory

We remember things in specifics, not generalities. If I asked you to remember a special summer vacation from your childhood, you would retrieve from your memory a bunch of mental snapshots and images—one special moment from the vacation, then another. Maybe the snapshots would include the moment when you and your girl-friend were down by the dock, sharing lunch, tossing pebbles in the water. The sun was pushing through an overcast sky. The air was humid. The trees and shrubs across the way were a deeper green than usual, still damp from the earlier thunderstorm. Snapshots: her smile, the kiss, your feet dangling in the water—a moment in time. And then you say to me, "Yeah, that was a great summer." It is impossible to remember the entire summer all at one time. Thoughts occur one after another, not all at the same time.

Understanding the way memory works is important to animators because there is a particular kind of expression on the face of a person who is remembering something. A bad actor "indicates" the act of remembering. He'll scratch his head, stroke his chin whiskers, and say, "Why, sure . . . I remember that summer. . . ." But when a person *really* remembers something, he doesn't do all that indicating. On the contrary, the act of remembering—especially something that is the deep past—tends to *still* a person, not animate him.

Not only does a face involved in memory become more still, the eyes shift in predictable ways. Let's say you have to animate a character that is remembering something from long ago, like maybe his childhood in the farmyard or school days in Minsk. When we remember something, we actually "see" it all over again, and it causes our eyeballs to do funny things. Try this experiment: Describe to me what you did when you got out of bed this morning. In your mind's eye, you will suddenly be transported to the perspective of a fly on the wall of your bedroom. You'll "see" yourself lying in bed, wak-

When you recall a recent memory, the eyes shift upward.

ing up, shifting your feet to the floor. Remember doing that? Good. Notice how, as you "saw" this memory, your eyes actually shifted off to the side and slightly upward? Well, they did. Try it on a friend. Recent memory causes the eyes to shift upward and to the side. More distant memory, like what the dashboard looked like on the first car you owned, will cause the eyes to shift downward and to the side. It's almost like the more distant the memory; the deeper into yourself you have to look to find it.

When you remember something, you do not continue to gaze straight ahead. I can tell you're skeptical about this, so don't take my word for it. Try it with a friend. Ask her to tell you about her Bat Mitzvah or something, get her to describe the room the party was in. Watch her eyes shift as she remembers.

When I'm teaching acting, I can always tell if a student if faking a memory sequence by the focus of his eyes. If he continues to stare straight out at the audience while he is remembering, then I know he is only *acting* like he is remembering. He's not doing the real McCoy.

Making certain that a character's eyes shift in the correct direction in the context of the memory is important. If you get it wrong, the audience will not catch the mistake. But they will know something is just not quite right. The moment doesn't ring true. Send the eyes in the wrong direction, and you'll be losing empathy.

The Use of Symbolism and Foreshadowing

A person watching a live-action movie will presume that 100 percent of what is on the screen means something. If you have a scene that takes place in a shack in the wilderness, the fellow in the audience will take notice if you include, for example, a small purple wildflower sitting in a water glass on the counter. He won't know what to make of it, but he will file it away in his brain just in case this is information he may need later on in the story.

This tendency for an audience member to endow every single thing on screen with importance is potentially a valuable tool for animators of both movies and games. You can use it to foreshadow events, to expose character traits, and to redirect or misdirect attention to plot.

The key to the use of symbols rests in the audience's inclination to endow absolutely everything on screen with importance. This is also the Achilles' heel of this tool, and it is why you must tread carefully. On a certain level, just about everything is a symbol of some kind. Words themselves are symbols. I say, "cat," and you get an image in your mind, a symbol. I give an on-screen character a kitchen knife, and it may or not be an important symbol. It could be that he wants to cut himself a chunk of parmigiano reggiano, or it could be that he is contemplating mayhem. It all depends on the story being told and the kinds of characters you have established.

The use of symbols and subliminal messages is actually an old Madison Avenue trick that probably was borrowed from stage plays and religious ceremonies. You can easily grasp its modern dynamic application by studying politicians during an election year. Notice how often they include the American flag in their public appearances. The flag is, of course, a powerful symbol. Position a short-sleeved George Bush in Yellowstone Park for a speech against the backdrop of Old Faithful, and he becomes an environmentalist (symbolically). Photo-ops are all about symbolism, in fact.

Symbols in stage plays are ancient. Stage designers make use of them all the time. I'll wager I have personally appeared in dozens of plays that had either phallic symbols or images of the Cross scattered around in nonobvious ways. Years ago, I directed a Murray Schisgal stage comedy entitled *Luv* in summer stock. It amused me to always cause the men in the cast to cross to the lone woman in the cast, instead of her crossing to them. I was real proud of myself because I figured this kind of blocking sent a subliminal message to the audience about how men in Schisgal's world were subordinate to the women. I figured nobody in the audience would ever consciously notice what I had done and, indeed, nobody ever did. Looking back on the production from my current perspective, I still think the blocking choice was interesting, but I'm not so certain it carried the symbolic wallop I intended. It may have been too subtle by half.

Screenwriters routinely use symbolism and foreshadowing to advance the plot. Hamlet's father appears as a ghost early in the famous play to inform him of his murder. Hamlet is enraged maybe to the point of insanity and we in the audience are set up to expect the worse. The ultimate goal with foreshadowing is to project the climax. You want the audience, at the moment of climax, to be totally surprised by what happens and yet to recognize that it was utterly predictable all along. Foreshadowing and the use of symbols are how you achieve this trick. Remember in *The Sixth Sense* when the kid says early on, "I see dead people"? That's foreshadowing.

Practical Application for Animators

First, symbols are fun, but the story is everything. Any symbolism or foreshadowing you use needs to be logical and consistent with the story. You can't take a lousy plot and fix it with symbols. In *The Iron Giant*, the refrains about the giant wanting to be Superman become symbolic after a while. Superman is a symbol of goodness, power, and self-determination. When the Giant flies into space at the end of the movie, on a collision course with the bomb, the last thing we hear him say is, "Superman. . . ." His destiny, foreshadowed earlier in the movie, has become reality.

Second, try to incorporate symbols into justifiable character behavior. Humans are wonderfully inconsistent at times, capable of multilayers and seemingly contradictory behavior. Hamlet has within him the makings of a future king and also the seeds of insanity. His father's ghost sets him off. Hitler reportedly had a genuine affection for children. The temptation, especially with game designers, is to create characters that are very mission-oriented. (This was, to me, a major failing in the movie *Final Fantasy*.) Being mission-oriented is a good thing up to a certain point, but you can generate more emotional depth in your game player if you allow the characters to occasionally exhibit behavior that isn't in pursuit of a huge goal. Remember Marlon Brando's flower garden in *The Godfather?* That garden, happy and frequently full of children, exposed a marvelous character element, it seems to me.

Finally, if you are in pursuit of an international audience, keep in mind that symbols are a cultural thing. An American flag means one thing in the United States, but it may mean something else entirely in China. Michael Dudok de Wit uses a universal symbol in his Academy Award–winning animation *Father and Daughter*. A bicycle is the same the world over. Keep an eye out for the most common denominator. This was, by the way, one of the great secrets of Charlie Chaplin's success. If you read his autobiography, you will learn that he was very conceptual about trying to come up with character behavior that would resonate internationally. He was looking for what is true of all humans.

Mirrors

Want to create a firestorm in a room full of animators? Walk in there and suggest that they get rid of their mirrors. Animators love mirrors! They like to make facial expressions in them, and act out scenes in front of them. Little mirrors, big mirrors, hand mirrors, full-length mirrors, animators will usually have one close at hand. Stage actors, by contrast, quickly learn to *avoid* mirrors. It's a left brain/right brain problem. As soon as you shift your brain into a watching mode, you stop acting. The moment you wanted to watch is gone, and a new moment has arrived. You wind up standing there with a silly expression on your face, in a freeze frame. What's going on? Are mirrors good or bad for acting? Useful or not? Rather than providing a hard-and-fast rule, running the risk of turning up the heat even further, let me simply offer a perspective that highlights one of the fundamental differences between the way that live actors and animators approach acting.

It is literally and physically impossible to be 100 percent actor and 100 percent audience simultaneously. The problem with acting into a mirror is that you are trying to force an impossible situation, splitting off part of your brain to watch what the reflection of what rest of you is doing. Since live actors aspire to be 100 percent "in the moment" when they act, rehearsing in front of a mirror is a path that leads in the wrong direction—duality. A century ago, philosopher Denis Diderot (1713–1784) wrote a famous treatise titled *The Paradox of the Actoring*, in which he asserted that all acting actually has this kind of duality, that no matter how much an actor tries, he can never be 100 percent "in the moment" (2000, 198–201). If he succeeded, blocking out all other conscious considerations, he might just wander off the stage or maybe hurt somebody in the big murder scene. Diderot correctly pointed out that an actor must always have a controlling distance from his performance. Indeed, an audience requires that the actor be in control of his performance. If the actor appears out of control on stage, it makes the audience nervous.

Diderot's theory of duality is the wiggle-room in which animators do their mirror thing. Animators do not have a live audience to give them immediate feedback, and so they act for the audience in their heads. Duality—doing and watching at the same time—works a lot better for animators than it does for actors.

Acting for the audience in your head

Mirrors are a good way for the animator to check and analyze poses, broad action, facial expression, that kind of thing—but you'll get into trouble if you try to actually act, "in the present moment" while watching yourself in the mirror. In other words, if you try to go through an entire full-body scene, for one thing, you will necessarily have your face turned toward the mirror so you can watch yourself, which may not be appropriate for the scene.

Stage actors are taught not to think about externals or "results." Facial expressions are "results." If I hit your toe with a hammer, you'll make a facial expression without thinking about it. If you sniff a vial of ammonia or a skunk in the woods, you'll make a face without thinking about it. An animator has a different kind of problem: He will say to himself, "My character smells a skunk. Now what kind of face would he make?"—at which point he gets out the mirror out of the desk drawer and wrinkles up his nose for inspection. An actor would consider this to be "indicating," or playing a "result." An actor would not say to himself, "I need to let the audience know I smell something bad . . . hmmmmm. . . . What kind of expression can I make? . . ." Instead, he would actually smell something, the air in the room probably, and play mental tricks on himself to pretend the smell is obnoxious.

The issue with mirrors, from an actor's perspective, is that if he watches himself in a mirror, he'll be tempted to re-create that look or expression on stage or in front of the movie camera. And that would not be acting at all, but a form of mimicry. ("Lessee . . . the bad odor facial expression goes like this.")

The proof for animators is in the pudding of course. Mirrors have been a valuable hand tool for many years, and if they work for you, then keep using them. But if you really want to see how facial expressions and body movement occur naturally, it would be better to videotape yourself acting out a scene, and then replay the tape for study. That would generally be too time consuming, right? So go ahead and use the mirror. But keep in mind the limitations.

The Form
9

Comedy

> The animator should know what creates laughter—why do things appeal to people as being funny.
>
> —Walt Disney memo to Don Graham December 23, 1935.

> If what you're doing is funny, you don't have to be funny doing it.
>
> —Charlie Chaplin

> There is only one way of making comedy richer—and, paradoxically, funnier—and that is by making it more serious.
>
> —Walter Kerr, *The Silent Clowns*

I confess that, as an actor, comedy is my Achilles' heel. I can be a funny guy on stage and, at times, I enjoy my own performance too much. Once I get an audience laughing, the temptation is to say to them, in effect, "Hell, if you think that was funny, take a look at this!"—at which point I try to top myself and, of course, the laughter dries right up. The audience doesn't like it if the actor laughs at himself or points too overtly to the joke. They want to participate, to use their imagination, and if the actor is telling them where the laughs are, they get insulted.

If you want to find the comedy in a scene, forget about being funny and ask yourself what is true. What is the scene really about? What do the characters want? Where is the negotiation? If you're trying to be funny, you're on the same slippery slope that carried the Keystone Kops into oblivion.

Lift the hood of any good comedy, and you'll find the engine of a good drama. This is why, when a person decides to become an actor, his training usually begins with drama, not comedy. Comedy is harder than drama. Comedy is drama exaggerated, heightened and enriched. The legend is that, on his deathbed, Noel Coward was asked if dying was hard. "No, dying is easy," he reportedly replied, "Comedy is hard."

I'm convinced that the training of new animators is made doubly difficult because so much of the stuff of animation is comedic, even farcical. The temptation is to begin acting training by analyzing what kind of movement is funny and why—as if the movement itself has inherent entertainment value. It is easy for the new animator to overlook the important correlation between comedy and drama. How many animators cut their teeth on an animated *Hamlet* or *The Merchant of Venice* after all?

Comedy is not a stand-alone form. It is a spin-off of tragedy. Before comedy, there was tragedy. Comedy came about when we decided to make fun of how serious we are. Laughter is actually an evasion of despair. (Warning! I'm about to get philosophical again!) We're all staring into the jaws of death, and we spend most of our lives trying

Comedy/drama are joined at the hip

not to think about it. Hence, we laugh. Ultimately, the joke is on us because we die anyway. Comedy looks the awful truth directly in the face and shrugs. Or spits. Or stamps its foot.

Former *New York Times* drama critic Walter Kerr, in his marvelous and essential book *Tragedy and Comedy* (now out of print, by the way) draws the line between comedy and drama by citing the ancient Greek tale of Oedipus, which is about a man who marries his mother and kills his father. When he realizes what he had done, he is so anguished that he puts out his own eyes and banishes himself into the desert. That's a tragedy. But if Oedipus, on his way out of town, passes another blind guy who has killed his father and married his mother, the situation becomes comedic. Why is that? Because we can't handle the idea of two Oedipuses! The awfulness and pain is too much to bear, and so we laugh. Walter Kerr wrote another wonderful book that happily is not out of print, entitled *The Silent Clowns*. It's all about Chaplin and Keaton and the gang, and is a must-read.

Playwright Neil Simon finds a dividing line between drama and comedy in a fight he had with his wife. They were living in New York on Central Park West, and they were having a fight while she was cooking dinner. He doesn't remember what the fight was about, but it doesn't matter. She was furious, so furious that when she took a package of frozen peas out of the freezer, she slammed it on the counter to emphasize her point. Just then, Simon recognized that what she was doing was drama. But, if she had taken that same package of peas and *thrown* it at him, it would have become comedy! At one level it is drama, but extended, heightened, it becomes comedy.

Charlie Chaplin, whose work I like to cite in my Acting for Animators classes, created a Little Tramp who was the ultimate optimist. No matter how many lemons life dealt him, he would make lemonade. But his optimism and cleverness would not be funny if he wasn't being optimistic in the face of death. Watch how he makes fun of the rich, most notably in *Modern Times*. Money won't buy you a seat in heaven.

Woody Allen, to name a modern-day counterpoint to Chaplin, is the ultimate pessimist. He wakes up every morning and confronts the cold reality of his ultimate demise. And then he lives the day the best way he can. When a car splashes him with a mud puddle, Woody figures that comes with the turf. If his wife runs off with another man, that is only to be expected. If he falls in love with another man's wife, well, why would nature not put him through such anguish? That's life.

The comedy of both Chaplin and Allen depend on them maintaining a certain perspective on human mortality. It is not simply that both men are funny to watch physically, though that is certainly true. Their movement is informed by their psychology. Chaplin has that spring in his step, always heading out for a brighter day. Woody Allen has high anxiety, angst, knowing that no matter what he says or does, it's going to be curtains sooner than he wants.

Comedy is drama—extended, heightened, enriched, and exaggerated. Any good comedy script, if acted slowly, will play as a drama. Neil Simon comedy will withstand this litmus test. Any good Disney comedy will play as a drama. Tragedy and comedy are bedmates. Charlie Chaplin was inspired by the infamous Donner Party with its rumored cannibalism and starvation when he came up with his shoe-eating sequence in *Gold Rush*.

In his book *Chuck Amuck*, Chuck Jones says that "comedy is unusual people in real situations; farce is real people in unusual situations" (1989, 142). I would add that all people are unusual, and all people are us. A good comedy character, regardless of the vehicle, is one we can identify with. If he is too oddball, we will distance ourselves from him.

Farce

Animation lends itself strongly to farce. When Wile E. Coyote tries to run through the cave entrance he painted on the side of the mountain, only to flatten himself against the rocks, that's farce. When Sylvester climbs up on the stool and finally gets access to Tweety's cage, only to discover a salivating bulldog where the bird ought to be, that's farce. When Bugs Bunny falls off the cliff, tumbles half a mile to the ground and is only punished with a spinning head, that's farce. When the Tasmanian Devil eats several sticks of dynamite, thinking they are a roast turkey, the resulting stomach explosion causes only indigestion and surprise, that's farce.

Mack Sennett's silent films, particularly the Keystone Kops series, were farce, as were some of the films of Buster Keaton and Charlie Chaplin. When the Little Tramp gets caught in the spinning cogs of the giant factory machine in *Modern Times*, that's farce. In reality, a person would surely die if he got sucked into the innards of a giant machine but, in farce, the characters rarely die. This is why animation is actually a better medium for comedy of this sort than live action is. In animation, you can crash cars harder, toss characters from greater heights, even have them get shot through with shotgun pellets—and still survive.

Another element of farce is that machines and mechanical devices are the enemy. Guns are likely to explode in the character's face, elevators are likely to go down when they should go up, airplanes will run out of gas at the most inopportune moment, and the electric razor will go nuts and shave a path across the top of the character's head. Farce is about mechanics, mechanical things gone wrong, timing, and the surprise element. Farce is definitely not the place to be worrying much about a lot of in-depth character analysis. Typically, characters in farce are pretty one-dimensional. Wile E. Coyote doesn't need any deeper character analysis. He's living in the desert, he's hungry, and food-on-the-run is nearby, a tasty Road Runner. Chaplin's character in *Modern Times* is just a workaday kind of guy, happy to have a gig, a full tummy, and a warm bed. When he gets accidentally swept up in labor protests, he doesn't even realize what is happening because he is completely uninformed about politics.

Caricature

You can hold a mirror up to everything in nature, in which case you have a photograph. Or you can hold a mirror up only to quirks, in which case you have caricature. Caricature, in a way, holds an imperfect mirror up to nature, emphasizing those aspects of reality that you, the artist, consider most important.

Annibale Carracci (1560–1609), a naturalistic draughtsman of the Bolognese School, was the world's first caricaturist. He explained his art this way: "Is not the caricaturist's task exactly the same as the classical artist's? Both see the lasting truth behind the surface of mere outward appearance. Both try to help nature accomplish its plan. The one may strive to visualize the perfect form and to realize it in his work, the other to grasp the perfect deformity, and thus reveal the very essence of a personality. A good caricature, like every work of art, is more true to life than reality itself" (Lambourne 1983, 7).

The important thing to realize about caricature is that, before you can caricature a character, you must first have a clear understanding of what the character is really like. It's that thing about comedy being drama extended. First ask what's true. Then enhance it.

The Medium
10

Video Games

Some of the most interesting and edgy work in animation is happening at video game companies, not movie studios. This $9 billion a year industry is financially neck-in-neck with the feature film business and is on a steady upward growth curve. I've taught for some of the biggest and most successful game companies and have been frankly impressed by their commitment to excellence and determination to improve the acting in their games.

It wasn't that long ago that most games were being developed to play exclusively on a computer, but it is clear that the future of games is on the Internet. Sony with its Playstation and Microsoft with its X-Box have both added features that allow the player to log on to the Internet for real-time play. The line between films, TV shows, and games is blurring. The marketing geniuses in the game industry have figured out that computer games tend to make the player physically lean in with head down, a posture that feels sort of like work instead of play. Video games that unfold on the living room TV, on the other hand, cause the player to physically lean back in a more playful posture. I realize this may sound simplistic and obvious, but decisions involving many millions of dollars are currently being based on just that kind of thing—leaning in or leaning out.

Movie companies want their movies to be made into games, and game companies want their games to be made into movies. This cross-over would seem to be a natural symmetry and is actually happening, but the results have more to do with marketing than anything else. Just as many novels do not easily lend themselves to film adaptation, many, if not most, movies do not easily lend themselves to game adaptation, and vice versa. The creative team responsible for the best selling game *Final*

The line between feature films, TV shows, and video games is blurring

Fantasy for instance produced a movie of the same name, but the movie became the mega-flop of 2001.

There are several major challenges for those who work to convert movies to games and games to movies. For one thing, the development cycle for a movie is shorter than that for a game. When movies and games of the same title are released simultaneously, it frequently means that the game has not had sufficient time to be developed. Still, box office strategies being what they are, a hit movie can sell a mediocre game.

And then there is the matter of aesthetics, which are very different in games than in movies. A good movie can deliver a wide spectrum of empathatic emotion to the viewer, but the essential element of a good game is the fun of game play. All else, including acting, is secondary. And anyway, it is virtually impossible to create in the game player the same feeling of empathy he might experience in a movie because an essential requirement for empathy is physical distance. In a video game, the viewer is actually a player in the game and is on stage.

It is self-evident that movies are made to be watched and games are made to be played, and although females are starting to show up in significant numbers on line playing puzzle-oriented games, the primary target audience for video games remains teenage boys, a group that craves a lot of action. When game producers insert too many cut-scenes (live action movie clips that invite a deeper emtional response) into the action of a game, they do so while risking that the footage will actually annoy the player. If he has to stop playing the game to watch a cut-scene, and if a cut-scene goes on too long, the player may become impatient.

More about empathy. An audience member watching a stage play or movie sits in her seat and has no control over what the characters on stage do. If the audience member could in any way affect the behavior of a character, this would kill any possibility of an empathic response. And as you have heard me say more than once in this book, the name of the game is to affect the audience on an emotional level. That means you need to generate a feeling of empathy. Video games have a huge obstacle to get across in this arena.

The emotional response that is evoked in many video games is basic fight-or-flight. It equates to an adrenaline rush and excitement, the video game equivalent of Mister Toad's Wild Ride. Your blood pressure rises as you shoot or broad-sword the other guy before he shoots or drop-kicks you, or before your car crashes into a building or hits a policeman. For sure, many games will continue to be developed along these lines because the market demands it. The improvement in them will be in character design and realism of game play.

Knowledgeable pros in the game industry precict that the next big artistic growth spurt in video games will be associated with the evolution of what movie directors know as secondary characters. Since the player is the primary actor on stage in a game, the development is going to be with the characters that the player associates and inter-acts with. For example, there are some games now in which the primary player has been given an animated companion with whom he develops a relationship. When the companion comes under threat in game play, the player must defend him. The player experiences a more complex emotional response in such an event, something beyond mere fight-or-flight. He feels affection for the friend. Very clever.

Regardless of the genre, game design is limited by available memory and the ren-dering speed of the computer. Realistic and multifaceted animation eats up a lot of memory. Where a feature film has a single story line that plays out in a linear fashion, a game may have many hundreds or even thousands of variables and situations, each dependent on how the player plays the game. Game designers and programmers can only work with the platform memory and rendering speed they have available to them of course, and economics dictate that there must be a limit to the detail that can be animated in any particular scene.

When I teach at game companies, I continually encounter a systemic division between the animators and the programmers. Animators are limited in their ability to give characters depth of emotion or behavior if the designers don't dictate and the programmers don't provide a flexible enough program. For example, when a character runs from point A to point B, the way he runs—from an acting perspective—depends on the circumstances of the scene. A character will run one way if he is chasing the bad guy or another way if he is running after his girlfriend. He will run yet another way if he is fleeing from a bad guy that is pursuing him or if he is searching for his dog. The animators may want to allow for this kind of variable, but if the programmers have given them only a single run-cycle to work with, then they are stuck with it. If the programmers dictate that a character must move in a particular way 100 percent of the time, then that is the end of the discussion. Animators necessarily work in tandem with designers and programmers.

Two things need to happen in order for the game industry to develop geometrically. First, the programmers need more memory to work with and, second, designers are going to have to work more closely with the animators. It appears that more memory is on the horizon though. I have, for example, heard serious talk about future Playstations having the capacity to hold as much as 2,000 pages of visual data or 37,000 hours of audio. Also, as more game players acquire broadband, the designers will be able to use the Internet itself to expand game play possibilities. As for the designers and animators working more closely with one another, this is something the industry will have to figure out. Designers and programmers tend to be "heady" people, very left brain; animators tend to be more artistic and emotional. It will be up to the managers of the companies to get these two essential sides of the creative equation into closer sync.

For the present—with no change in organizational structure and no increase in available memory—there is still room for improved performance animation in video games. The seven acting principles I outlined at the beginning of this book all apply to games, with the variable being the mechanisms of empathy. Let me reiterate some principles and techniques that might be particularly useful to game animators and designers:

1. Scenes begin in the middle; they don't begin at the beginning. Your character was someplace else before she entered the scene and will be going someplace else when she exits the scene.

2. Play an action until something happens to make you play a different action. A typical situation in which this principle can apply is a scene in which characters are waiting for the arrival of the game player. From the player's perspective, the action proceeds down a hallway or something, and then the player enters a room or area of some kind. It is an acting error to have the waiting characters simply be waiting in a wait-cycle. The characters were doing something before the arrival of the player. The player's arrival interrupts whatever they were doing and spins their reaction in a new direction.

3. Gestures do not necessarily have to be an illustration of the spoken word. Try to use psychological gestures when you can.

4. A character should react to the reality of whatever the other characters are doing. If for instance you have two characters standing side-by-side and shooting at the enemy, and Character #2 gets wounded, then you need to have Character #1 react to it or acknowledge it. The reaction may not be as profound as it might be if you were animating a movie, but there should be *some* reaction, maybe a flinch or recoil or something like that.

5. Comedy rests on the tension between man's possibilities and his limitations. In the movie *Titanic*, Leonardo DeCaprio exults at the prow of the ship, "I'm king of the world!" That is a majestic moment full of possibilities for him in life. If his pants had suddenly unsnapped and fallen to his ankles, the moment would have become comic. The pants would say to him, in effect, "You may be king, but you still have to wear pants!" If you want to set up a gag in a game, keep it simple. You won't have time to do much more than that anyway. Set up a character to behave with bravado and then have him trip over his own shoelaces. You can study Charlie Chaplin for clues about how to make this work. He was a master of it.

One of the most promising acting developments that I have seen in games is character associations and buddy systems. The player will be given an animated companion of some kind with whom he develops a relationship. Then the companion comes under threat in game play, so the player must defend him. The player feels a complex emotion in such an event, something beyond mere fight-or-flight. He feels affection for the friend. It is a kind of empathic response that doesn't require the player to be sitting in the audience watching a scene. Very clever.

Television Commercials

The United States is the Big Kahuna of consumer societies. Americans sell things to one another, and television commercials are the main aortic valve to the sales monster. It is a misnomer to say that a television program is "sponsored by" this or that advertiser. Television shows exist in order to deliver good-humored consumers to the commercials, not the other way around. More correctly, the commercials are sponsored by the shows! Ever since the game show scandals in the 1950s, advertising on television programs has been sold magazine-style, and the contest among producers in Hollywood has been to see who can deliver the most valuable demographics as measured by age and spending habits. Presently, the most desirable television viewer is young, maybe 18 to 28 years old, and female because she has plenty of money and is a fickle, style-conscious, impulse shopper. She'll go see the same movie ten times, will buy whatever CD is hot this month, and will make the fashion designer or clothing store exec of the moment oil-sultan rich.

Though television commercials have long featured clever and famous animated characters such as Speedy Alka Seltzer and the Pillsbury Dough Boy, current spots are hitting an astonishingly high standard, equivalent to the best production value of feature films. Tippett Studio, the academy award–winning Berkeley-based visual effects company, produced its first TV commercial in 2003, for Blockbuster Video Stores, feature a couple of funny CG gerbil-like furry characters named Carl and Ray. Framestore CFC in the UK has produced a series of jaw-dropping special-effect spots for Levi's jeans and Johnny Walker Red Whisky. In one, live-action actors are running through walls and racing up tree trunks and, in the other, a school of dolphins morphs into schooling and swimming humans.

Computer animation has broadened production possibilities at the same time that the attention span of the average viewer is shrinking.

1. Implied Visual Message

Television commercials are not about information. In fact, *Consumer Reports* did a study and discovered that only one commercial in eighteen conveys any useful information at all. They're not about information; they're about emotion. The idea is to create a positive emotional association with the product. The implied visual message is, "If I use this product, I will be like the person in the commercial" (i.e., "I will have a lovely family, plenty of sex and money, lots of laughs, and maybe a Pillsbury Dough Boy to play with!"). In the world of television advertising, nobody dies, nobody ever gets any diseases that can't be cured by a nonprescription drug, and all the kids are cute. Animated critters such as roaches, fleas, ticks, and flies die in commercials, but theirs is most often a farcical, going-down-in-flames kind of death.

2. No New Products

There really are not any new products under the sun. When someone finally invents a cure for cancer, nobody will have to do any commercials for it. Cars are pretty much the same and they all fall apart at about 100,000 miles, pain relievers are pretty much the same, McDonalds and Burger King are pretty much the same. The strategy behind most commercials is to get the consumer to buy product A instead of product B on the premise that she will buy something of that product genre anyway. (More than 60 percent of television advertising is targeted at the female consumer.) We want her to buy Tide instead of Ivory Snow, a Lexus instead of a Mercedes, Haagen-Dazs Ice Cream instead of Ben & Jerry's.

3. No Conflict

The situations in television commercials are not to be confused with those in movies or theatre. We have already talked about how a scene is a negotiation, but in commercials this is not always the case. Commercials have close to zero conflict. There are no real negatives in most commercials, no possibility of losing in a negotiation. It's a happy-go-lucky world. Remember the movie *The Truman Show?* Pretty much on target if you ask me.

4. Pictures—Not Words

One of the first things I teach actors who want to learn how to act in commercials is to start watching them with the sound turned off. The real power of television commercials is in the visuals. We're back again to the fact that our sense of sight is more powerful than our sense of hearing. This is the secret to political advertising. Doesn't matter what the politico is saying, just as long as he's kissing babies and standing in front of the American flag.

5. Playing to the Camera

In movies and television shows, it is unusual for the character, animated or otherwise, to speak directly to the camera. Mickey Mouse used to do it on the old Mickey Mouse Show, but you rarely see it these days. Speaking directly to the camera is known, in acting terms, as *breaking the fourth wall*. In other words, the standard relationship between the audience and the show on television is static. The viewer watches as the action unfolds but doesn't interact with the characters. If a character speaks directly into the camera, he is speaking directly on a one-to-one basis to each individual viewer who is watching the show on television. He pulls the viewer into the action, makes him an actor in the show.

There is a trick to speaking directly and dynamically to the camera: You—or your character—should talk to the camera as if it is a person who might talk back. A monologue is actually a duologue. It is impossible to talk to "America." Even if 40 million people are watching a commercial, they are 40 million individual people, each of whom must think your character is talking directly to him.

When we talk to another person, we tend to watch that person's face to see if he is following us. That is because conversation is hierarchical. We make a point and then, when that point is grasped, we can add more information on top of it, building steadily toward a final point. When we watch the other person, our own face tends to animate. Eyebrows lift, eyes widen. For proof of this, set up your video camera and practice talking *at* it. Then talk *with* it, as if it is a person who might talk back.

This business of talking *with* rather than *at* is important and bears reiterating. The temptation an animator has is to make the character cute, cuddly, or whatever. But if you want to really connect with your audience one-to-one, you need to make the facial expressions interactive.

I wrote a book for actors titled *The Audition Book: Winning Strategies for Breaking into Theatre, Film, and Television* that contains a lengthy chapter on the world of commercials. Many of the techniques used by live actors in commercials can be applied to animation, and I recommend you read the book.

Classroom Exercises 11

Classroom improvisation games are designed to stretch your acting muscles. It is like going to a gym and working out. Today you work on your arms and tomorrow on your thighs. Games should be fun and carefree. Animators that participate in them should not be made to feel that they must entertain anybody. Classroom exercises of this sort are not about being funny. They are about paying attention to your own processes.

Power Center Games

When I teach Acting for Animators, I always include *power center games*. I ask two students to come to the front of the room and face one another, standing twenty feet apart or so. The exercise develops in three stages. First, the students walk forward and pass one another as they would in the hallway at work. They greet one another, "Hello." The point of this is that the students be aware of where their normal power center is. It is located just below the navel usually. Once we have established this point of focus, I begin to move the power center around on their bodies. I ask them to think of it like a balloon that can have different properties. The balloon can be very light or very heavy, and it can push or pull. The idea is to let the power center initiate the movement in the body. If, for instance, I tell an animator to put her power center in her nose, she should let her nose pull her across the room. Her body will follow her nose. Or if I suggest that the power center is in the small of the back, pushing, then the student should let her body be pushed along, like in a stiff wind storm. I continue this until the two students have got the point and until the animators that are observing can see the physical impact of shifting a power center. Then, I move along to *status negotiations*. The same students who are doing the power center shifts now become *master and slave*. They cross in the hall and greet one another as master and slave. Almost automatically, the student playing the slave will lean forward, throwing his power center into the floor. I point out what is happening. We continue with these exercises as long as students in the class want to do them.

Note to teachers: Many of your animators will not want to get up and do these exercises. I strongly advise that you not make them do it if they don't want to. The exercises are designed to benefit those watching as much as those participating. An unwilling student will simply be too nervous to learn anything anyway. It is better to let such a person sit and watch and maybe sketch postures and such.

Animal Exercises

To do this exercise properly, the students really ought to visit a zoo or somehow study animal behavior. The exercise will work without that preparation, but it will be better if based on direct observation. Here's how the exercise works: Picture a watering hole in Africa, on a hot day. The only water for miles around is in this hole. Animals that might normally be enemies put aside their instincts to fight and drink side by side. Now, all the animators in the room will pretend to be an animal. Pick one, and let's get started.

"What kind of animal would my character be if my character were an animal?" This is an excellent rehearsal technique, and you'd be surprised how it can stimulate you emotionally to take on animal qualities. Stanley Kawalski in Tennessee Williams' *Streetcar Named Desire* is a barely disguised ape. Observe his low power center, his animal awareness of the world around him, his preference for physical action rather than words. Same with Schwarzeneggar's characters, for the most part, and Sylvester Stallone's Rocky. Alma, in Williams' play, *Summer and Smoke* is a bird. So is the young woman in William Mastrosimone's *The Woolgatherer*.

For animators who may very well be animating an animal in the first place, the equation can work the other way. "What kind of a human would my animal be?"

What Is My Profession?
What Is My Age?

Viola Spolin, the mother of the improv group Second City, wrote a marvelous book, *Improvisation*. It includes lots of theatre games for the theatre, and improvs designed to loosen up the actor's "instrument." One of the games in the book is good for animators to learn, and I try to include it when I teach. Here's the set-up: There's a bus stop, a bench. Everybody in the class picks a profession and one by one, they go up and wait for the bus. The idea is to avoid showing the audience what profession has been chosen. Just wait for the bus. You would be amazed at how little you have to do in order to communicate a chosen profession to the audience. One day, I saw an animator go wait for the bus, sitting quietly, evidently lost in some lovely, rhythmic thought. "You're a composer, a musician," said someone in the class. The animator was shocked because that was precisely what she had chosen and she was doing virtually nothing but listening to music in her mind. Audiences are smart creatures. You don't have to hit them over the head. Now try the same exercise, selecting age instead of profession.

Given Circumstances Game

When you do something like enter a room, you know (1) where you are, (2) what is happening, and (3) why it is happening. Simple, right? You'd be surprised how a simple thing like this can trip up beginning actors and animators. The temptation is to do things in order to be amusing. Stick with concrete circumstances, and it will work better, trust me.

I like to get animators up and on their feet for this exercise: I give everybody in the class the following script and then send them up on stage, two at a time. (On the CD-ROM that accompanies this book, you'll find this exercise performed three different times by two actors from my acting class in San Francisco.)

> PERSON #1: Good morning.
> PERSON #2: What's so good about it?
> PERSON #1: Did you sleep well last night?
> PERSON #2: You know damned well how I slept.

PERSON #1: Is there anything for breakfast?
PERSON #2: Fix it yourself.
PERSON #1: Listen, I think we ought to talk about this.
PERSON #2: I think that's a very good idea.

The object of the exercise is to change the given circumstances. Person #1, for example, might enter the room in a great mood, happy as a lark because he just got word that he was accepted to grad school. Person #2 didn't sleep well last night because Person #1 was snoring. So Person #1 has no idea why Person #2 is in a sour mood and has to react to that. Or Person #1 may be operating on the presumption that it isn't morning at all, but afternoon. Maybe he's joking when he says "Good morning." And Person #2 has to play off the reality of whatever Person #1 brings into the room.

Suppose Person #1 had a bad night and Person #2 had a great night? Person #1 enters with a hangover, say, seeking some coffee. Person #2 is playful. Look at the script again. The lines belonging to Person #2 may, at first glance, seen confrontational. Not necessarily. They may very well be playful. Depends on the given circumstances. Maybe Person #2 was kept up all night by Person #1's amorous advances. It was a night like no other, one for the record books. Person #2 is energized; Person #1 is pooped. This game can go on for hours if the players are inventive. Person #1 just won the lottery; Person #2 is pregnant. Person #1 has decided to move to Paris; Person #1 gambled away the family savings last night. And on and on and on.

Gibberish Exercise

The students will crack one another up with this game. The point of it is to get them to trust their impulses instead of relying on their logistical reasoning skills. One student gives a lecture or demonstrates a product, in gibberish, nonsense talk, while another student "interprets" for him. Pretend it is a speech at the United Nations. The speaker's language is intelligible, without interpretation. The value in this exercise is that it teaches the importance of intention and highlights the relatively less important value of the words themselves.

Boss and Workers Game

Three people are involved. Set up three chairs on stage, side-by-side. The boss sits in the middle chair, and two workers sit on either side. When the boss talks to the worker on his right, the worker on his left makes faces at him. When he talks to the worker on his left, the worker on the right makes faces at him. If the boss catches one of the workers making a face at him, he "fires" him. The fired worker goes back to the audience, and is replaced by another worker.

The interesting thing about this super-fun game is that it works best when the worker who is making faces really exaggerates things. He stands on his chair, waves perspiration odor at the boss, that kind of thing. It is hysterically funny to watch the offending worker try to act casual when he has been almost caught in the act of making faces.

The Iron Giant:
An Acting
Analysis
12

The Iron Giant, directed by Brad Bird, is a magnificent achievement in American animation. I had nothing whatsoever to do with the production of this film and, as of this writing, have never even met Brad Bird. But I am so enthusiastic about its merits that I want every reader of this book to see it, to study it for the acting lessons it contains. To that end, I am providing the following acting analysis of a few scenes from the movie. There is no scientific basis for my selection, only personal inclination. When something jumped out at me, acting-wise, I wrote it down to share with you. The scenes are titled as you will find them in the published DVD, which is generally available for purchase or rental.

Before examining the scenes, keep in mind a couple of overall notes. I told you about the value of "adrenaline moments," remember? In The Iron Giant, scene after scene is an adrenaline moment. The way to judge whether a scene fits the criteria is to ask yourself if it is likely that the characters in the scene will remember the scene when they are in their old age. "Oh yeah, that was the day I met your mom, Hogarth. That damned squirrel climbed up my pants leg, and we had havoc in that diner. Heh, heh."

Second, I have repeatedly spoken of the importance of establishing a sense of empathy. The Iron Giant does that in spades. I have attempted to point out some of the techniques that were used to create the reaction.

Now, to the scenes.

Scene 2: "Squirrelly at the Diner"

Hogarth Hughes has captured a squirrel and wants to keep it as a pet. As the scene begins, he is pedaling through the seaside town of Rockwell (as in Norman Rockwell, I am sure. Cute.), Maine on his bicycle, in transit to his mother's place of employment, the local diner.

ACTING NOTE #1—The dock workers are minor players, extras in the scene, but notice that each of them is engaged in specific chores. Each is pursuing an objective. One fellow is moving boxes, another is coiling rope, and two others are collaborating on opening a container.

ACTING NOTE #2—As Hogarth enters the diner, he passes a man wearing a hat, sitting at the counter, reading a newspaper. Notice that the man mouths the words as he reads. Excellent character observation. Haven't we all seen people do that?

ACTING NOTE #3—Hogarth meets Dean for the first time, telling him that the squirrel has escaped and has run under his table. Significantly, the first time we—the audience—see Dean, he is asleep, still holding the newspaper, with its bold headlines about the Russian Satellite, in his hands. This conveys a lot of information. First, Dean is following current events. He's literate. Second, he's a "night person," in contrast to everybody else in the diner. It is likely that he is eating breakfast after working all night. Note his day-old beard. And the sunglasses suggest that he's not a fan of bright light. His clothing is black, in contrast to the typical earth tones worn by everybody else. He's a nonconformist.

ACTING NOTE #4—The squirrel crawls up Dean's pant leg just as Hogarth's mother, Annie, approaches the table. Note how Dean at first successfully hides the discomfort of the squirrel in his pants, trying to be a good friend to Hogarth. The rule of acting is "play an action until something happens to make you play a different action." The squirrel going up the pant leg is the motivation for a new action. What Dean does about it is to "cover," to try to downplay the tickling going on down there. Following the same acting principle, the squirrel finally reaches Dean's crotch level, motivating him to stand up, unzip his pants, and release havoc into the diner.

Scene 4: "An Iron Giant"

The Iron Giant tries to eat the local power station, and Hogarth saves his life.

ACTING NOTE #1—The first time we see the Giant, he is searching for food. He's hungry. This is a point of empathy because humans act to survive. We all have to eat. So, immediately, we can identify with a primal need in the creature.

Scene 7: "Something Big"

We meet Kent Manseley from the U.S. Government for the first time. Note that his power center is in his chin.

ACTING NOTE #1—After Manseley is shown the ruins of the power tower and scoffed at the suggestion that a "giant monster" may be responsible, he is asked which part of the U.S. Government he represents. Immediately after the editing cut from the close-up of Manseley to a long shot of him and Marvin the worker, he assumes a performance mode. Notice how he rocks first back on his feet and then struts forward, putting on a show for Marvin, trying to intimidate and impress him. That backward rocking is different from the way other characters begin their walks, and it suggests a person who likes to be on stage, who is full of himself.

ACTING NOTE #2—Manseley turns into a coward when he discovers the monster has eaten half of his car. Note how his rhythm and power center shift. When he drags Marvin out of the woods to see the car, notice how he is leaning forward, power going into the ground, low-status to Marvin, who now seems to be the Rock of Gibraltar. Notice how his arms begin to wildly gesticulate. The "performance" he was doing for Marvin only moments before is totally eradicated, the mask has fallen, and the "real" Kent Manseley stands before us. Brilliant.

Scene 8: "The Luckiest Kid"

Hogarth gets to know his new friend.

ACTING NOTE #1—Here is where we first start feeling real empathy for the giant. Note that, in his first appearance in the scene, he is very robotlike, stomping toward Hogarth in a manner that could mean doom for the boy. When they finally come face-to-face, the interaction begins. The Giant, with great effort, imitates the sitting posture of the boy. Clearly, sitting in this way is not a normal movement for the Giant. He sort of collapses onto the ground. He's trying to be friendly, and we empathize.

ACTING NOTE #2—After the Giant gives Hogarth the power station shut-off switch, thereby expressing his gratitude for Hogarth having saved his life, we get a close-up of the Giant's head. Note the way he tilts his head to the left, almost puppylike. Again, we relate to his efforts to be friendly. The tilt of the head expresses curiosity, eagerness to learn.

ACTING NOTE #3—When the Giant makes a first effort to speak, saying "Blah, Blah, Blah," he rocks his head back and forth. Talking is fun! Like a game of "fetch!" We can relate. The important thing is in the rocking of the head.

ACTING NOTE #4—After the Giant distinguishes between a rock and a tree, Hogarth gets excited about being "the luckiest kid in America." Note the Giant's physical reaction to Hogarth's obvious delight. The Giant doesn't know what everybody is so happy about, but he's happy to be happy, too!

Scene 9: "Train Coming"

ACTING NOTE #1—The Giant starts dozing off when Hogarth is so long-winded. Another point of empathy. The Giant needs not only to eat, but also to sleep, in order to survive. We can relate. Perhaps as important is that the Giant is already learning good manners. Rather than go to sleep, which he could easily do, he wakes himself back up so he can continue to be a good audience for Hogarth. Who among us has not done that at the most boring parties in the world? More empathy.

ACTING NOTE #2—After the Giant tries to eat the railroad track, the crossing signal begins to ring and blink the red light. It happens quickly, but note the Giant's reaction. He drops the track from his mouth and switches his playful attention to the crossing signal. A new toy! More empathy. The Giant is an overgrown cross between a child and a puppy, it seems.

ACTING NOTE #3—The Giant puts the broken train track back together again. Rather than simply have him do the chore, the animators went for the playful game approach. The Giant is eager to do his master's bidding, to please Hogarth. He wants to get the tracks back together "just right," and so he frets over it until it is too late, and he is hit by the train. This is an important moment in the story because, later, we will learn that the Giant has a true talent for arts and crafts. Again, we can relate to the idea of perfectionism.

Scene 11: "Hands-On"

ACTING NOTE #1—Hogarth's blessing of dinner is a marvelous 45-seconds of animation. Acting-wise, the thing that makes it interesting is that he has to play two actions at once: (1) protecting the Giant's hand from being discovered and (2) saying grace. In terms of priority, it is more important for Hogarth—as it would be for any child— to protect the Giant's hand. And so, saying grace becomes an action in pursuit of a double objective. The swinging pendulum of the grandfather clock on the wall, near the dinner table, is important, too. The steady tick-tock rhythm of the pendulum contrasts with, and highlights, Hogarth's inner rhythm, which is near panic.

ACTING NOTE #2—Chet Mansely leers at Hogarth's mother in a frankly sexual way. Hogarth notices this, setting up the competition between the boy and the government agent. It's primal. Hogarth is the man of the house now that his father is dead, even if his functions do not manifest themselves in a sexual way. Mansely is, from the first instance, an interloper. Later on, we will see Mansely literally sitting in Hogarth's father's favorite easy chair and in his place at the breakfast table. This is very smart story telling, to have the competition between Hogarth and Mansely function on multiple levels, one of them primal.

Scene 15: "We Like Dean"

ACTING NOTE #1—The Giant eats a car, and the burglar alarm goes off. Under pressure to silence it, he goes through a decision-making process. There are a couple of acting notes in this moment. (1) Emotion leads to action. (Thinking leads to conclusions.) Because the Giant must silence the alarm quickly, the solution springs from emotion. (2) When a character is indecisive, it is best to have him go from specific to specific in his thinking. Note how the Giant considers various options for silencing the alarm. He looks to his right ("Is there something over there I can use to silence it? No."). He looks to his left ("Is there something over there, then? No."). He looks down, getting the idea to sit on the car. It is a one-two-three-step mental process, very specific. (This also creates ever more identity with the audience of thinking, emotional humans.) When sitting on the car doesn't work, the Giant tries to silence it by hammering on it. (I actually did that once with a car alarm. Didn't work for me either.) Finally, he figures out the best solution, one which uses his super strength. He throws the car some miles out into the ocean.

ACTING NOTE #2—Hogarth's case of the coffee jitters is an excellent sequence. The acting note has to do with the effect of external substances, such as—in this case— caffeine. What you do is allow the substance to have the physical effect (nervousness, quicker rhythms, racing mind), and then you act to control it. As wired as Hogarth is, he is not grasping at his heart or getting afraid. Instead, he tries to behave with Dean as if this is perfectly normal. Dean sees right through it, of course. Another nice thing about this sequence is that Hogarth learns a lesson in life ("too much coffee will make you nervous") from Dean who will, later in the story, begin to become a true father figure.

Scene 16: "Fast Friends"

ACTING NOTE #1—Mansely's manic side surfaces at the soda fountain. Note how his body rhythm changes and the arms gesticulate. It's become a pattern now that we can recognize, and from which we can draw conclusions about Mansely's strengths and weaknesses. Anxiety is a high power center. See how the arms are flailing around the head? Also, note that Mansely is stooped over when he goes into his Sputnik tirade. Logically, the stoop is motivated by his desire to get eye-to-eye with Hogarth but, in a status transaction—which is the acting lesson—that kind of stoop comes across as low-status, unpowerful. Mansely's manic quality is his Achilles' heel, the thing that ultimately will sink him.

Scene 20: "Soulful Under the Stars"

ACTING NOTE #1—The scene with the deer in the woods strikes all kinds of emotional chords, of course—Bambi and ET most notably. How delighted the Giant is when he gets his first good look at the pretty deer! A new playmate! More empathy. The gently offered finger of friendship, followed by a gunshot.

ACTING NOTE #2—The Giant is depressed and, as he lies in the junkyard that night, notice how physically heavy he is, how much effort it takes to move a finger. Gravity is almost too much to overcome. Death equates to gravity. That's probably why they call them "graves."

Scene 23: "Weapons to Bear"

ACTING NOTE #1—After the Giant almost kills Hogarth, Dean accuses him of being a "big gun." The Giant says, "I am not a gun." Note how his hands are palms-up, submissive. The psychological gesture says, "I won't hurt you."

Scene 24: "I Am Not a Gun"

ACTING NOTE #1—The Giant saves the two boys who fall off a building in town, much to the gratitude of the townsfolk. When Hogarth and Dean arrive on the scene, the Giant picks up Hogarth and, once again, says, "I am not a gun." This time his body language expresses confidence, assurance. No turned out palms. The Giant has chosen what he wants to be, and he is decidedly not a gun. The energy has returned to his body; he has overcome gravity and death.

Scene 26: "Arsenals Unleashed"

The Giant's transformation from grieving friend, when he believes that Hogarth has been killed, to a fighting machine, is accomplished by removing all of the vestiges of humanity that have been carefully layered on his character. As a weapon, he is thoughtlessly, automatically, knee-jerk reactive to assault. No compassion, no emotion, just killing. The Giant's movements lose their grace. Now he moves like a recoiling rifle.

Scene 28: "The Giant's Choice"

ACTING NOTE #1—As was the situation when the Giant tried to decide how to make the car alarm stop sounding in an earlier scene, he now goes through a far more complex decision-making process. Still, acting-wise, the thoughts are specific. When Hogarth tells him that, when the missile comes back to earth, "we will all die," the Giant stands erect and gazes at the townspeople gathered together like so many deer in the woods. The Giant looks upward, his gaze following the trajectory of the missile. The decision is made. When he crouches to tell Hogarth good-bye, he has become more human than any of us— gentle and caring. He makes a joke, cheering up Hogarth. "Me go. You stay. No follow."

Postscript: What Is Method Acting?

The average person on the street has heard of Method Acting, and, as I mentioned at the beginning of this book, one of the first questions I was asked at PDI was about Method Acting.

The favored acting style of the mid-ninteenth century essentially amounted to posturing. Actors did not try to experience real emotion on stage, but to show the audience how it would look if they did experience real emotion. You've seen the drawings and photographs of those old-school actors haven't you? Actresses in swoon postures, actors displaying mock anger, silly-looking stuff. There were books written, in fact, with drawings of the various poses and emotions that actors were supposed to imitate.

Then came an amateur Russian actor named Constantin Stanislavsky who got mightily impressed with research being done by Sigmund Freud and Pavlov. Those men were mapping the human emotions, getting into things like conditioned response. Pavlov did his famous experiment of ringing the bell whenever he fed the dog. After a while, he only had to ring the bell and the dog would salivate. Stanislavsky was fascinated and figured actors ought to be able to use these new ideas. Why couldn't actors ring a bell and have their mouths water? Why must actors pretend to have emotion on stage when they might experience the real McCoy?

And so, on June 23, 1897, Constantin Stanislavsky met in a Moscow restaurant with producer/director Nemerovich Denchenko to discuss the formation of a new theater and acting school—a school that would apply this new thinking about psychology.

The main focus of Stanislavsky's early work with his actors at the new Moscow Arts Theatre was the search for emotional *triggers*—memories, smells, sights—whatever would stimulate true emotion in the actor. The actors applied their new skills to productions of plays by a new playwright, Anton Chekhov. And the rest, as they say. . . .

When the actors from the Moscow Art Theatre performed in New York in 1922 American actors picked up the Stanislavsky approach. In particular, Lee Strasberg, later known at the originator of Method Acting, adopted and expanded on Stanislavsky's ideas. He and a few other very serious theater folk formed the Group Theatre in New York, and Strasberg conducted regular acting classes for the resident company of actors. Later, after the dissolution of the Group Theatre, Strasberg headed up the Actor's Studio, from whence sprang Marlon Brando, James Dean, Paul Newman, Al Pacino, and a host of other well-known actors.

Most actors today have been trained in the principles first laid down by Stanislavsky, though there are variations, and many have been taught in offshoots from Strasberg's work. Some teachers put more emphasis on development of the imagination, some put more on the search for emotional triggers, but, one way or another, it all goes back to Pavlov's dog. Actors are always trying to get their mouths to water on cue.

Recommended Reading and Additional Study

Recommended Reading

There are probably thousands of acting books in print and at least dozens at any halfway decent bookstore. You probably won't hurt yourself by reading any of them. Terms may vary from text to text—*emotional recall* in one book will be called *affective memory* in the next, that kind of thing—but it is pretty much all in pursuit of naturalistic, psychologically truthful performance. If you were to get hold of something experimental, like say Brecht or Grotowski, you'll know it right away.

My short list would include

On the Technique of Acting by Michael Chekhov

On Acting by Sanford Meisner

Respect for Acting and *A Challenge for the Actor* by Uta Hagen

Strasberg at the Actor's Studio edited by Robert H. Hethmon

Impro by Keith Johnstone

Acting: The First Six Lessons by Richard Boleslavsky

Laban for Actors and Dancers by Jean Newlove

Preparing a Character and *An Actor Prepares* by Constantin Stanislavsky

Virtual Humans: A Build-It-Yourself Kit Complete with Software and Step-By-Step Instructions by Peter Plantec

Laban Movement Schools

For further Laban study

Jean Newlove Centre for Laban Studies
Flat 1, 44 Woodville Gardens
London W52LQ
Fax: +44 (0) 181 997 3007
Email: jean@newlovemakepeace.demon.co.uk

Laban/Bartenieff Institute of Movement Studies
520 8th Ave, Suite 304
New York, NY 10018
(212) 643-8888

Leslie Bishko
Emily Carr Institute of Art and Design
1399 Johnston Street
Vancouver, BC Canada

Laban Books

Your Move: A New Approach to the Study of Movement and Dance by Ann Hutchinson Guest (Gordon and Breach, 1983)

Laban for Actors and Dancers by Jean Newlove (Routledge, 1993)

The Mastery of Movement "(2nd ed.) by Rudolf Laban, revised by Lisa Ullmann (Macdonald and Evans, Ltd., 1960)

Choreutics by Rudolf Laban, edited by Lisa Ullman (Macdonald and Evans, Ltd., 1966)

Body Movement: Coping with the Environment by Imgard Bartenieff (Gordon Breach Science Publishers, 1980)

Phrasing and Effort: Significant Components of Dance Dynamics by Vera Maletic (Ohio State University, 1984)

Works Cited

Bishko, Leslie. 1999. Conversation with author about Laban Movement Theory, October.

Blair, Preston. 1990. *How to Animate Film Cartoons*. Laguna Hills, CA: Walter Foster Publishing.

Blum, Deborah. 1998. "Face It." *Psychology Today* (Sept./Oct.): 32.

Brook, Peter. 1987. *The Shifting Point*. New York: Theatre Communications Group.

Chekhov, Michael. 1985. "Lessons for the Professional Actor," in *Performing Arts Journal*, 129.

————. 1991. *On the Technique of Acting*. New York: HarperCollins.

Crafton, Donald. 1982. *Before Mickey—The Animated Film*. Cambridge, MA: MIT Press.

Culhane, Shamus. 1990. *Animation from Script to Screen*. New York: St. Martin's Press.

————. 1998. *Talking Animals and Other People*. New York: Da Capo.

Diderot, Denis. 2000. "The Paradox of Acting." In *Theatre Theory Theatre: The Major Critical Texts*, edited by Daniel Gerould. New York: Applause Books.

Ekman, Paul. 2003. *Emotions Revealed*. New York: Tims Books.

Ekman, Paul, and Wallace Friesen. 1975. *Unmasking the Face*. Upper Saddle River, NJ: Prentice-Hall.

Ekman, Paul, R. W. Levenson, and W. V. Friesen. 1983. "Autonomic Nervous System Activity Distinguishes Between Emotions." *Science* 221: 1208–10.

Ekman, Paul, and Maureen O'Sullivan. 1991. "Facial Expression: Methods, Means, and Moues." In *Fundamentals of Nonverbal Behavior*, edited by R. S. Feldman and B. Rime. New York: Cambridge University Press.

Gallwey, W. Timothy. 1974. *The Inner Game of Tennis*. New York: Random House.

Gladwell, Malcolm. 2002. "The Naked Face." *The New Yorker*, August 5.

Hall, Edward T. 1969. *The Hidden Dimension*. New York: Doubleday.

Hooks, Ed. 2000 [1996]. *The Audition Book: Winning Strategies for Breaking into Theatre, Film, and Television*. rev. ed. New York: Watson-Guptill.

Johnstone, Keith. 1981. *Impro: Improvisation and the Theatre*. New York: Routledge.

Jones, Chuck. 1989. *Chuck Amuck*. New York: Farrar, Straus & Giroux.

Kazan, Elia. 1988. *A Life*. New York: Alfred A. Knopf.

Kerr, Walter. 1990 [1975]. *The Silent Clowns*. rev. ed. New York: De Capo.

Lambourne, Lionel. 1983. *Caricature*. London: Her Majesty's Stationery Office.

Maletic, Vera. 1984. *Phrasing and Effort: Significant Components of Dance Dynamics*. Columbus: Ohio State University Press.

Menache, Alberto. 2000. *Understanding Motion Capture for Computer Animation and Video Games*. San Francisco: Morgan Kaufmann.

Merritt, Russell, and J. B. Kaufman. 2000. *Walt in Wonderland: The Silent Films of Walt Disney*. Baltimore: Johns Hopkins University Press.

Newlove, Jean. 1993. *Laban for Actors and Dancers*. New York: Routledge.

Robinson, David. 1985. *Chaplin: His Life and Art*. New York: McGraw-Hill.

Spolin, Viola. 1999. *Improvisation for the Theatre: A Handbook of Teaching and Directing Techniques*. 3d ed. Evanston, IL: Northwestern University Press.

Sweet, Jeffrey. 1993. *The Dramatist's Toolkit: The Craft of the Working Playwright*. Portsmouth, NH: Heinemann.

Thomas, Frank, and Ollie Johnston. 1981. *The Illusion of Life: Disney Animation*. New York: Hyperion.

———. 1993. *The Disney Villain*. New York: Hyperion.

Wright, Robert. 1994. *The Moral Animal*. New York: Pantheon.

About the CD

This CD contains video clips illustrating seven essential acting concepts that are discussed in the book, as well as the various "efforts" (how an actor moves through space) delineated by Rudolf Laban. It is designed to offer actual demonstrations of the principles addressed in the book. In addition, on-screen text helps guide you through the demonstrations and further expand upon the principles involved.

To use the CD, simply insert it into the CD-ROM drive on your computer. The CD should launch automatically and allow you to navigate through the improvisations and the demonstrations.

Systems Requirements:

Windows/PC

Pentium Processor (233 Mhz or higher)

Windows 95 (or higher)

64 MB RAM (more recommended)

SVGA Color Display (or better)

8x CD-ROM Drive (or faster)

Macintosh

PowerPC Processor

System 8 (or higher)

64 MB RAM (more recommended)

SVGA Color Display (or better)

8x CD-ROM Drive (or faster)